Teachers as Agents of Change:

A New Look at School Improvement

Allan A. Glatthorn

Robert M. McClure
NEA Mastery In Learning Consortium
NEA National Center for Innovation
Series Editor

nea PROFESSIONAL LIBRARY
National Education Association
Washington, D.C.

THE AUTHOR

Allan A. Glatthorn is Associate Dean of Graduate Studies at the School of Education at East Carolina University in Greenville, North Carolina.

Dr. Glatthorn taught education courses at the University of Pennsylvania in Philadelphia for 14 years. Before that, he was a high school principal for six years and a high school teacher for 20 years.

Copyright © 1992
National Education Association of the United States

Print History
  First Printing: October 1992
  Second Printing: October 1993

Note

The opinions expressed in this publication should not be construed as representing the policy or position of the National Education Association. Materials published by the NEA Professional Library are intended to be discussion documents for educators who are concerned with specialized interests of the profession.

Library of Congress Cataloging-in-Publication Data

Glatthorn, Allan A., 1924–
    Teachers as agents of change: a new look at school improvement /
  by Allan A. Glatthorn.
        p.   cm. — (NEA school restructuring series)
      Includes bibliographical references (p).
      ISBN 0-8106-1853-2
      1. School management and organization—United States.
    2. Classroom management—United States.   3. Education—United
    States—Aims and objectives.   I. Title.   II. Series.
    LB2805.G536   1992
    371.2'0973—dc20

                                        92-26974
                                        CIP

CONTENTS

THE CONTEXTUAL ELEMENTS

FOREWORD

In 1985, when my colleagues and I began the Mastery In Learning Project, we set out to explore several assumptions about how schools could change and improve. Among these was a commitment to faculty-led change; the centrality of the teaching and learning interaction to school quality; and the absolute necessity to attend to the conditions or contexts that surround teachers, principals, and students. In this book, I am delighted to say, the author, in exceptional detail, takes us through the elements of change in a way that will be helpful to practitioners.

This business about improving schools has received a lot of attention since the mid-eighties. We have learned how very difficult and complex it is to change schools. We have learned that shifting the structures has to be preceded by significant shifts in the way we think about learning, teaching, and curriculum. And, we have learned how critical the teacher is to this process.

This book extends our understandings of change. More importantly, in a practical way, it helps teachers to become involved in shaping their schools in the very ways they want to be involved: by attending closely to teachers, curriculum, and the learning of their students.

—Robert McClure
Series Editor Director
Mastery In Learning Consortium
NEA National Center for Innovation

PREFACE

This book is addressed chiefly to teachers, although I hope that administrators and supervisors will read and use it. It represents my attempt to make sense of a growing body of research on what really counts in school improvement—and on how the teacher needs to become a key agent in the process.

I wrote it out of a 45-year commitment to the profession—as a classroom teacher, school principal, central office supervisor, and university professor. During the course of my experience, I have come to have a high regard for the teaching profession; in a sense, this book is my tribute to its members.

While I am deeply indebted to the thousands of teachers whom I have known and worked with, I wish to acknowledge a special indebtedness to some who were particularly instrumental in my growth: G. Michael Davis, Charles R. Coble, Lynn Bradshaw, Billy Revels, Peter Grande, Elizabeth Thomas, Sharon Schlegel, and Charles Watson. I also feel a special indebtedness to my colleagues in the Massachusetts Commonwealth Leadership Academy, who during recent years have been a continuing source of growth for me. Finally, I owe more than I choose to acknowledge to my wife, Barbara Glatthorn, and my children (Carol, Dale, Laura, Louise, and Gwen), who in their own ways are all great teachers of the young.

Like all authors, I have profited from good editorial work; the editorial staff of the National Education Association was at all times helpful and supportive.

You will notice that I have chosen to write in a direct style, using both first and second personal pronouns; I want to get beyond the professional jargon that often impedes good communication and write as if I were speaking to you.

—Allan A. Glatthorn

Chapter 1

LAYING THE GROUNDWORK FOR SCHOOL IMPROVEMENT

You and your colleagues across the nation have become, understandably, somewhat cynical about much of the rhetoric of school reform. There are several reasons for such cynicism. Too much of that loose talk is a thinly disguised attack upon teachers. Too much of it recommends a top-down approach to school improvement that begins with input from the superintendent or the principal and ends with the classroom teacher. Too much of it is foolishly cast in terms of competing with Japan. And too much of the rhetoric seems to be an excuse for not providing the money that educators need to do the job.

This book hopes to take an approach that will make such cynicism less justified. It begins with the assumption that you and your colleagues are competent and committed professionals who have chosen education as a profession because you want a better world for the children and youth you teach. It is based upon a sincere conviction that you and your colleagues should be the key players in school improvement, not the passive recipients of someone else's bright ideas. It ignores the issue of competing with Japan; all of us want the best schools that this nation needs, not the schools that Japan seems to need. And it frankly admits that schools are like the defense establishment in one important way: you can't buy good education (or good defense) on the cheap. While the book does not deal directly with the issue of providing additional funds, it assumes that people who are sincere about improving education will realize that quality education requires significant funding.

Its central thesis is that teacher empowerment begins with teacher knowledge. Teacher-involvement in decision-making and school management is of little value if teachers are not informed and aware. The book then is a tool for empowering you, by providing you with the best available research on what really counts in school improvement and what is only rhetoric.

ONE MODEL OF SCHOOL IMPROVEMENT

Let's begin with the big picture, so that the individual parts that follow will make coherent sense. The model shown in Figure 1-1 represents my attempt to synthesize a large body of research on school effectiveness; the chief sources are noted briefly below the figure and fully in the reference list at the end of the chapter. The model is described in this chapter and then used to provide an organizing structure for the rest of the book. It should be emphasized that this model is not the best model or the right model; it is simply my attempt to make sense of the research by portraying the key elements as I see them. In fact, I would encourage you and your colleagues to develop your own model.

THE ESSENTIAL ELEMENT: EFFECTIVE CLASSROOMS

There is one essential element of school improvement—effective classrooms. The classroom is where it all begins. Unlike some earlier versions of school improvement that minimized the importance of the classroom, this book argues that the individual classroom is the key component. Consider the conclusion reached by Edward Pauly in his book, *The Classroom Crucible* (1991).

> . . . the underlying cause of the failure of school reform efforts is (the establishment of) education policies that depend on schoolwide prescriptions and uniform compliance from teachers and students, when the reality of schooling is that all classrooms are different. (p. 34)

Another piece of telling evidence relative to the importance of the classroom is the research on educational

10

Figure 1-1
ONE MODEL OF SCHOOL IMPROVEMENT

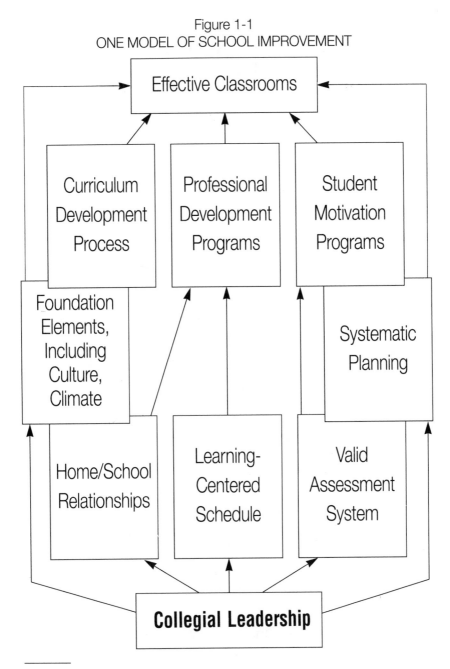

SOURCES: Cotton, 1990; Duttweiler, 1988; Fraser, Walberg, Welch, and Hattie, 1987; Fullan, 1990; Purkey and Smith, 1985; Wayson, 1988.

productivity. An analysis of 3,000 studies of educational research (Fraser, Walberg, Welch, and Hattie 1987) showed that nine factors increase learning. Those nine factors can be grouped into the following three categories:

Student Aptitude

1. Student ability or prior achievement

2. Student development, as indicated by age

3. Student motivation

Instruction

4. The amount of time students are engaged in learning

5. The quality of instruction and curriculum

Psychological Environments

6. The home "curriculum"

7. The classroom environment

8. The peer group outside the school

9. Minimum leisure-time television viewing

There are two main points to emphasize about this list. The first is to note that several of these factors lie outside your control: student ability, student development, the home curriculum, the peer group outside of school, and the amount of leisure television viewing that students do.

All the rest are chiefly classroom factors: student motivation, amount of time students engage in learning, the quality of instruction and curriculum, and the classroom environment. In summary, the factors that the school can control are classroom factors.

This does not mean, obviously, that the school district and the school do not count. As Fullan, Bennett, and Rolheiser-Bennett (1990) note, the teacher plays a key role in linking classroom improvement with school improvement. And Cotton (1990) provides evidence that effective districts are needed to support school improvement.

What is that effective classroom like? Briefly, it is a place where five crucial elements are present: excellent teaching, a meaningful curriculum, a supportive yet demanding classroom climate, quality time, and success-motivated students. Each of these is discussed at length in Chapter 2.

THE SUPPORTIVE ELEMENTS

The supportive elements are those components that directly affect and impact upon those effective classrooms. There are three supportive elements that enable the effective classroom to flourish. The first is an interactive curriculum-development process that gives due recognition to the school district's need for coordination and articulation, while giving classroom teachers considerable input into the curriculum and providing them with meaningful autonomy about the curriculum of their classrooms. It also maintains a clear and continuing focus on educational goals, or *exit outcomes*, to use the term favored by advocates of outcomes-based education.

The second supportive element is ongoing, high-quality professional development of the instructional staff in a supportive professional working environment. That professional development includes teacher-centered staff development and teacher-directed supervision. Rather than continuing to use outmoded, top-down approaches of clinical supervision, this book argues for a collegial, teacher-driven model that reduces the emphasis on accountability and increases the emphasis on growth.

The final supportive element is a set of systematic programs to enhance student motivation. Student motivation is so critical that it cannot be left to chance. You cannot actually

13

motivate students, of course. Motivation is an internal drive to achieve. However, you can provide the conditions in which student motivation is more likely to increase.

These three supportive elements are explained in Chapters 3, 4, and 5.

THE FACILITATIVE ELEMENTS

The three facilitative elements are once-removed from the classroom. While they are important, they do not have the immediate impact of the supportive elements.

The first is effective home-community-school relationships—an interactive process built upon the realization that the home, the community, and the school are partners, not adversaries, in the education of children and youth. Included in those relationships are the effective use of community resources as a means of expanding the school's resource base and the effective use of homework as a key component in developing home-school relationships.

The second facilitative element is a learning-centered schedule—one that makes the best use of human resources, that groups students effectively for learning, and that allocates time to reflect instructional priorities. While some so-called experts depreciate the importance of the school schedule as simply a "technical" matter, this book argues that it plays a key element in the learning process. As a consequence, teachers should have considerable input in developing the school schedule.

The third facilitative element is a valid and comprehensive assessment system. To be valid, it must use sound criteria and authentic measures. To be comprehensive, it must include student evaluation, teacher evaluation, leadership evaluation, and program evaluation. Evaluation data play a critical role in the entire school improvement and problem solving processes.

These three facilitative elements are examined at length in Chapters 6, 7, and 8.

THE CONTEXTUAL ELEMENTS

Surrounding all of the above are the vital elements of the school context, which provide a protective and supportive environment for the classroom.

The first component of the context is what is termed here the *foundation elements*, chiefly the school's culture and climate. The culture includes a pervasive set of values; for example, the importance of high expectations for all, the centrality of learning, the power of collegiality, and the need for continuing improvement. Those values produce a supportive school climate. In this climate several critical characteristics are present, such as a safe, orderly, and well-maintained environment and a sense of community. Other foundation elements include norms of behavior, the hallmarks of culture, the mission, the vision, and the goals.

The second element of the school context is collegial leadership. While earlier research speaks of the principal as the instructional leader, more recent research indicates that team leadership has a greater and more lasting impact. While the principal needs to play a major role, he or she should be leading a collaborative team effort that marshals the best efforts of all concerned.

The final contextual element is systematic planning for school improvement—an incremental planning process that uses school-developed data, identifies and solves emerging problems, and moves the school toward excellence.

The three contextual elements are addressed in Chapters 9, 10, and 11.

WHO DOES THE WORK?

Who does all the work involved in implementing the model? I am an unabashed advocate of three kinds of cooperative teamwork for this: teamwork between school administrators and teachers, between the school and the home, and among teachers who work together in instructional teams.

Between School Administrators and Teachers

The research is clear that schools achieve lasting and significant improvement when school administrators and teachers work closely together. While the focus of this book is on the teacher, the hope is that teachers and administrators have found ways of collaborating effectively, while recognizing the fact that at times they may hold differing views on key issues.

At this juncture you should keep in mind the research on the role that teachers' professional groups and unions play in school-improvement efforts. At times the popular press and some ill-advised administrator journals portray these groups as obstacles to change. The evidence is otherwise.

At the national level, both the National Education Association and the American Federation of Teachers have played an active professional role in advancing the agenda for school improvement. The NEA Mastery in Learning project is one such example (McClure 1991).

At the state level, several state affiliates have sponsored their own initiatives, while maintaining an understandable emphasis on better salaries and improved working conditions.

And at the local level, the evidence is clear and persuasive that teacher unions and professional groups do not represent an obstacle to improvement; in several instances, in fact, they have played an instrumental role in advancing new approaches to teacher development and evaluation. As a result, most teachers, even the most militant ones, do not see any conflict between being a good teacher and being a very active union member. Such teachers, even though frequently involved in conflict with their administrators, report being highly satisfied with their jobs (Kerchner 1986).

16

Between School and Home

The second type of collaboration is that between the school and the home. If you look back at the nine factors identified earlier in the chapter, note that two of them directly involve the home. The first is what the researchers call the "home curriculum," the extent to which the parents provide a supportive learning environment. And the second is the amount of television viewing that students do. By working closely and cooperatively with parents, you can make an impact on those two factors.

Among Teachers in Instructional Teams

The third type of collaboration is collaboration among teachers who are members of the same instructional teams. As will be emphasized throughout this book, teachers who work together in collaborative teams can have a greater impact than teachers working on their own. There is a price to pay, of course, for such collaboration: it takes time and effort if it is to be successful. But cooperatively generated improvement is worth the costs involved.

If you lack administrator support and cannot find the time to work with colleagues, do you give up? The answer here is a clear and strong no. You can find many suggestions in this book that you can carry out on your own. Working on your own to bring about small improvements is a better answer than giving up and doing business as usual. Teaching is a draining and taxing profession; teaching without hope is the road to despair.

FOR FURTHER READING

Cotton, K. 1990 update. *Effective schooling practices: A research synthesis.* Portland, Ore.: Northwest Regional Educational Laboratory. Offers a very useful synthesis of the research on effective schools.

Duttweiler, P.C. 1988. *Organizing for excellence.* Austin, Tex.: Southwest Educational Development Laboratory. Provides several focused chapters on the critical elements of effective schools.

Pauly, E. 1991. *The classroom crucible.* New York: Basic Books. Provides a scholarly but highly readable analysis of why the individual classroom should be the focus of improvement efforts.

REFERENCES

Cotton, K. 1990 update. *Effective schooling practices: A research synthesis.* Portland, OR: Northwest Regional Educational Laboratory.

Duttweiler, P.C. 1988. *Organizing for excellence.* Austin, Tex: Southwest Educational Development Laboratory.

Fraser, B.J.; Walberg, H.J.; Welch, W.W.; and Hattie, J.A. 1987. Syntheses of educational productivity research. *International Journal of Education,* vol. 11, 145-252.

Fullan, M.G. 1990. Change processes in secondary schools: Toward a more fundamental agenda. In *The contexts of teaching in secondary schools: Teachers' realities;* eds. M.W. McLaughlin, J.E. Talbert, and N.Bascia; 222–55. New York: Teachers College Press.

Fullan, M.G.; Bennett, B.; and Rolheiser-Bennett, C. 1990. Linking classroom and school improvement. *Educational Leadership* 47(8) 13–19.

Kerchner, C.T. 1986. Union-made teaching: The effects of labor relations on teacher work. *Review of Research in Education* 13:ISSUE: 317–52.

McClure, R.M. 1991. Individual growth and institutional renewal. In *Staff development for education in the 90s,* 2d ed., eds. A. Lieberman and L. Miller, 221–42. New York: Teachers College Press.

Pauly, E. 1991. *The classroom crucible.* New York: Basic Books.

Purkey, S. and Smith, M. 1985. School reform: The district policy implications of the effective schools literature. *Elementary School Journal,* vol. 85, 353–90.

Wayson, W.W. 1988. *Up from excellence: The impact of the excellence movement on schools.* Bloomington, Ind.: Phi Delta Kappa Educational Foundation.

Chapter 2

EFFECTIVE CLASSROOMS

Let's start by examining in detail what an effective classroom looks like. In doing so, I want to take a fresh look at the research and present a perspective that might be somewhat different from the usual ones. You've heard all about *time-on-task* and *anticipatory sets;* there is no need to re-examine these perspectives. Instead, this chapter will present a current research-based look at teaching, curriculum, classroom climate, time, and student motivation.

EXCELLENT TEACHING

To understand the nature of excellent teaching, think of teaching as craft, science, and art.

The Craft of Teaching

The craft of teaching, as the term is used here, encompasses the basics of effective instruction: the minimum skills that all teachers should have mastered. Figure 2-1 is one such formulation; there are, of course, several other such lists, which vary only in terminology and inclusiveness. These craft skills generally apply to all grade levels, all students, and all subjects; in this sense, they are generic. The craft is best learned through apprenticeships, in which student teachers, interns, and novice teachers learn under the direction of a skilled mentor. The essential criterion of judging the craft of teaching is utility: Does it work?

Despite the widespread acceptance of such lists of the essentials, many experts have raised serious questions about their formulation and use. They point out, first of all, that most of the research supporting the essential skills is correlational, not causal. For example, the research can explain that classes with high time-on-task are also classes with high achievement; but the

Figure 2-1
THE ESSENTIAL SKILLS OF TEACHING

LESSON CONTENT

1. Chooses lesson content that relates directly to curriculum goals, is appropriate in relation to student development, and corresponds with assessment measures.
2. Presents content in a manner that demonstrates mastery of subject matter.

CLIMATE

3. Creates a desirable learning environment that reflects appropriate discipline, supports instructional purposes, and helps keep students on task.
4. Communicates realistically high expectations for students.
5. Uses instructional time efficiently, allocating most of the time to high quality curriculum-related instruction and appropriate pacing.

INSTRUCTION

6. Provides an organizing structure for classroom work, presents a basic overview, specifies objectives, gives clear directions, makes effective transitions, summarizes material, reviews material, and makes relevant homework assignments.
7. Uses learning activities that are appropriate for the objectives and reflect sound learning theory; explains, demonstrates, and provides guided and independent practice when appropriate.
8. Ensures active student participation.

ASSESSMENT AND COMMUNICATION

9. Monitors student learning, uses this evaluative data to adjust instruction to meet individual needs, and gives students feedback about learning.
10. Explains clearly, questions effectively, and responds appropriately to students.

(Based on Glatthorn 1990.)

research has not established a causal relationship for that single factor.

The critics of these formulations also note that the essential skills are too often presented out of context. Generated chiefly from studies of elementary reading and mathematics instruction, the studies do not speak to the special problems of teaching advanced physics at the high school level, for example.

A third criticism is that such lists seem to support a teacher-centered model of direct instruction. Some 20 models of teaching have been identified by Joyce and Weil (1986), and most do not conform to the "essential skills" formulations without a great deal of modification.

Finally, the critics are concerned that using those essential skills to evaluate and supervise all teachers ignores the very different developmental needs of teachers; it does not make sense to ask a competent experienced teacher to continue to focus on the basics (Brophy and Good 1986).

If we see the essential skills as only the basic part of good teaching, and if we use them judiciously, then perhaps we can avoid the problems we just discussed.

The Science of Teaching

The science of teaching, as the term is used here, includes the advanced skills of teaching that have a sound basis in two kinds of research: the research scholars have generated in their carefully controlled studies and the research that you have done in teaching, reflecting about your teaching, and analyzing its meaning for you and your students. Both kinds of research are important. The scholars produce generalizations that apply across many classroom settings; you produce findings that make sense to you and your colleagues in teaching the students in your school.

Unlike the craft (which includes the generic skills), the science of teaching takes into consideration the special elements of the classroom context: the special students, a particular grade level, and one subject. It also draws from models of teaching other than the direct instruction model. In judging the science of teaching, the key criterion is validity: Are the skills supported by sound research?

The science of teaching can best be developed through research and dialogue: you and your colleagues review the research, reflect about your experience, and develop your own integration of empirical and personal knowing.

Figure 2-2 shows one formulation I have developed of the science of teaching writing at the high school level. It represents a synthesis of current research on teaching writing and draws from my own experience in that field.

The Art of Teaching

The art of teaching is the use of creativity in producing original and high quality learning experiences. The art goes far beyond the basics and builds upon the science. It is the expression of your creative intuition—an expression that seems to defy formulaic descriptions. However, by drawing from the research on creativity in the professions, some significant elements of the art can be identified.

It first of all involves your vision of the teacher you want to be, the image you have of yourself as teacher when feeling at your best. It also involves the use of your own creative intuition, when you draw from the depths of your experience and improvise. Surprisingly, perhaps, it seems to involve a sense of humor—the ability to laugh at yourself, at everyday classroom predicaments, and at the absurdities of how some aspects of schools are administered. There is a considerable body of evidence that creativity and humor are closely related.

The art of teaching also involves risk-taking and improvisation. The teacher as artist does not feel captured by formulas and lesson plans, but is able to take risks and improvise on the spot. Finally, it must include a sense of conscience—a conscience about the profession you have chosen, about the

22

Figure 2-2
THE SCIENCE OF TEACHING HIGH SCHOOL WRITING

1. Provide all students with effective instruction and opportunities for writing in a variety of modes and to a variety of audiences.

2. Provide a supportive writing environment; one in which writing is valued as a way of knowing and communicating, in which cooperation is valued as a means of learning, and in which oral language and dialogue provide a foundation for the writing experience.

3. Emphasize writing for real audiences and real purposes; minimize contrived themes and compositions.

4. Teach students to use the writing process flexibly; to adjust the time devoted to pre-writing activity and revision according to the communication context.

5. Teach students the thinking and problem-solving skills they need to write effectively.

6. Provide students with the *scaffolding*, the structure and the support they need to learn to write effectively, but gradually turn over control to them.

7. Encourage the use of and provide opportunities for peer feedback throughout the writing process.

8. Provide frequent opportunities for sharing and publishing writing.

9. Teach students the importance of revising; teach them how to do it and provide them with many opportunities to practice the skill.

10. Emphasize writing as an important skill to be used in many disciplines, not just in language arts.

11. Teach students how to use the technology necessary to retrieve information, to communicate with each other, and to facilitate the writing process.

(Primary sources: Applebee 1986, Dyson and Freedman 1991, Hillocks 1986.)

students you are trying to reach, and about the public issues that confront you and your colleagues as teachers and citizens.

The chief criterion in judging the art of teaching is aesthetic quality: Has the teacher fashioned a high quality and original learning experience that appeals and excites? The art of teaching cannot be taught; it can be nurtured, however, by supportive colleagues in an open and creative environment.

Putting It All Together

Here then is one picture of excellent teaching that integrates craft, science, and art.

> The teacher has mastered and internalized the craft. He or she uses the essential skills almost automatically in organizing the classroom. The teacher draws every day from the science of teaching in choosing methods and materials. From time to time he or she functions as a true artist, drawing from intuition, taking risks, and creating quality learning.

How can you develop your own craft, science, and art? That is the focus of Chapter 4.

A MEANINGFUL CURRICULUM

One of the correlates of excellent teaching is a meaningful and challenging curriculum. Consider whether the following picture presents an image of the quality curriculum you would like to produce.

First, it is a high quality curriculum for all students. Gifted students will master it in short order and move ahead at their own pace into greater depth and enrichment; students with learning problems will need more time and special help. But all students, regardless of ability, have equal access to quality. As a professional, you ensure that all students—regardless of ability, career plans, or school attended—experience a challenging curriculum that equips them for rewarding careers and further education.

Second, it is an articulated and coordinated curriculum. It is articulated in the sense that what is taught in Grade 5 acknowledges and builds upon what was learned in Grades 1–4 and provides a foundation for Grade 6. It is coordinated in the sense that what is taught in science relates to and uses what is taught in mathematics. (A fragmented and disjointed curriculum impedes learning.)

Third, it is a curriculum that emphasizes knowledge-based problem solving. Rather than teaching isolated critical thinking skills (such as drawing inferences), you first help students acquire a sound and deep knowledge base. Students cannot think critically about what they do not know; they cannot solve problems in science unless they understand science. However, that knowledge base is generative, not inert: students use that knowledge to solve meaningful complex problems. You act as a "cognitive coach," modeling, explaining, giving suggestions, and providing just enough structure to help them succeed. And you give special emphasis to specific thinking skills when they are needed in the problem-solving process.

Fourth, it is a curriculum that is appropriately integrated in three respects. To begin with, you integrate into all appropriate subjects the learning, writing, and reading skills that are the essential tools for acquiring knowledge and solving problems. Also, you integrate knowledge and skills within a subject, emphasizing the connections and interrelationships of each discipline, rather than teaching separate unconnected components. Finally, where appropriate, you cooperate with colleagues in integrating two or more subjects, such as English language arts and social studies.

While the current interest in interdisciplinary integration is in general a healthy development, you should keep in mind the caution advanced by Brophy and Alleman (1991): Many integrated units seem to be a collection of interesting activities that lack challenge and purpose. In other words, integration should be a means, not an end.

Next, it is a curriculum that is goal-focused. All components of the curriculum (the K–12 curriculum guide, the guide for one grade level, the teaching units, and the daily lessons) are organized so that they contribute directly to the educational goals or *exit outcomes* of schooling.

Finally, it is a curriculum that is multiethnic and multicultural, while giving due attention to the common culture that all students need to know. To what extent the curriculum gives special attention to the culture of minority groups in the school is a matter so controversial and complex that it needs to be resolved at the local level, with considerable input from parents, administrators, teachers, and scholars in the field.

However, you and your colleagues might consider the following guidelines for a curriculum that maximizes understanding for all, while minimizing divisiveness and controversy.

- *Equity.* Provide a high quality curriculum for all students, regardless of their ethnicity. Ensure that all subjects are based upon a curriculum that is accurate, emphasizes problem-solving, and provides a deep knowledge base.

- *Acceptance.* In social studies, use world history, anthropology, and U.S. history to foster acceptance of different cultures and perspectives. Provide all students with a global perspective that derives from a broad knowledge of world cultures. Emphasize the concepts of *culture* and *ethnicity* to ensure that students understand that all cultures are functional for their members— there are no superior or inferior cultures.

- *Power.* Help all students understand the pernicious effects of prejudice and racism by studying in depth these issues from both a global and an American perspective. Help them understand that prejudice and discrimination are destructive forces in every society—and that they are part of this nation's unfinished agenda. Help them develop the skills they need to deal with prejudice as they encounter it individually and as they experience it in the political arena.

26

- *Interdependency.* Use the social studies to emphasize the interdependency of all people in this modern age: understanding the Japanese culture is an act of self-interest. Enable students to see television broadcasts and to read newspapers from other nations so that they understand how other nations view the United States.

- *Accommodation without Assimilation.* Help minority students to function effectively in two cultures—their own and that of the dominant society. Give them many opportunities to study and value their own culture and its traditions. At the same time, develop in them the skills, knowledge, and attitudes they need to succeed in the dominant culture.

- *Expansion.* Provide all students with a curriculum that will expand their horizons. Encourage them all to learn a second language, as they progress in their native language. Help all students escape the limits of their everyday lives through a challenging science and mathematics curriculum that reflects their everyday world and gives them the skills they need to succeed in the twenty-first century.

In Chapter 3 you will find some specific suggestions to help you and your colleagues play a key role in developing and implementing such a curriculum.

A SUPPORTIVE CLASSROOM CLIMATE

High quality teaching of a high quality curriculum requires a supportive classroom climate. The specific nature of that climate will vary somewhat, depending upon such factors as your teaching style, the age and background of your students, and the subject or subjects you teach. The best climate for poor minority kindergarteners who are learning to read is probably not the best climate for affluent high school students who are studying calculus.

Given that caution, the following guidelines should help you reflect on the type of classroom climate you want to produce.

1. *The emotional climate is moderately warm.* Classrooms that are emotionally cold create barriers for many students, especially at-risk students; they are more likely to feel unwelcome and unaccepted by teachers who appear remote and uninvolved. On the other hand, classrooms that are emotionally hot are disconcerting for many students and violate the norm of appropriate distance between teacher and students. Often, in "hot" classrooms so much time is spent nurturing personal relationships that achievement suffers.

2. *There is a sense of order and seriousness of purpose.* The teacher has established and reinforces useful routines for such matters as starting class, checking homework, changing group structure, and collecting papers. Together the teacher and the students have established and continue to enforce rules for moving, speaking, and showing respect. The teacher knows how to prevent major discipline problems by making instruction exciting and by enabling all students to earn success. He or she deals promptly and effectively with any minor infractions.

3. *The classroom is success-oriented.* You should convey reasonably high expectations for all students. However, you should challenge the popular claims that most teachers have inaccurate and low expectations for students. As Good and Brophy (1987) note, studies of this issue conclude that teachers' perceptions of students are largely accurate, teachers form their judgments on the best available information, and most inaccuracies are corrected when better information becomes available.

Also, be somewhat skeptical about all the well-intentioned rhetoric about improving students' self-esteem. While the research in general suggests that self-esteem and academic achievement are related, many experts now believe that earned achievement results in enhanced self-esteem—not the other way around (Holly 1987). If you want to improve your students' self-esteem, help them earn meaningful success; do not give them unwarranted and excessive praise (Good and Brophy 1987).

QUALITY TIME

Quality time is classroom time in which all students are engaged in learning something new and meaningful—and doing so in a manner that keeps them interested in and involved with the learning task. The concern for quality time tries to get beyond the conventional wisdom of time-on-task and asks you to focus instead on the quality of the learning experience. Obviously, it is a good idea to keep students on task and not to waste excessive time before, during, and after instruction. However, there is a question that is more important to ask than"How much time are students spending on the learning task?" That question is instead, "What is the quality of the learning task?"

Consider these two scenarios: In Class 1, students spend a great deal of time doing textbook exercises. Because the teacher monitors their behavior closely, they seem to have high levels of on-task behavior. In Class 2, students are working in cooperative groups, solving complex problems. The teacher tolerates some off-task behavior as a way of reducing the stress of group competition. There is less time on task in Class 2, but better learning is taking place.

Obviously, you want both high time on task and quality learning, but your chief concern should be with the quality of the learning experience and the significance of the learning outcome. At the end of a class, ask yourself and your students the following questions:

- What did students learn by the end of this period that they did not know when they entered the classroom today?

- How significant was that learning? Was it significant in relation to their personal needs, their future learning, current educational goals, and the nature of that subject?

29

- How many students mastered that learning?

- Were the learning processes sufficiently engaging, meaningful, and challenging to keep students involved in the learning task?

- In general, was time used productively and effectively?

The intent here is not to suggest that all learning has to be exciting and personally relevant. It is to suggest instead that you keep in mind that learning time is finite, that some content is important and some is trivial, and that good teachers can make seemingly dull content challenging and stimulating.

MOTIVATED STUDENTS

The final and in some ways most essential element of effective classrooms is motivated students. As was noted in Chapter 1, motivation is an internal drive to achieve. In this sense you cannot motivate someone else. All you can do is create the conditions under which the motivation to learn is more likely to flourish.

While there are some useful motivation skills you can teach, the attitudes that students have seem to be much more critical. Listed below are the attitudes that, according to the research, are those possessed by highly motivated people; they are worded as students' statements so that you can put them on the bulletin board if you wish (Ames and Ames 1984).

- *I want to learn because I want to succeed in life.* My teachers are here to help me, but I learn for my sake, not for theirs.

- *Learning requires both ability and effort.* I can develop my abilities with my teachers' help; but I must put forth the effort.

- *I can make a difference.* I can achieve my goals, can influence what happens to me, and can determine the course of my life. I am not a helpless, passive person.

- *I am responsible for my actions.* I have it in my power to succeed or fail. If I fail, I will get the help I need and study harder next time; I will not blame other people or find excuses for my own failures.

- *I will work to achieve success, not try to avoid failure.* I will take risks as needed, will accept challenges, and will work toward the goals I have set.

- *I will work hard to learn because I want to be successful, not because I want to get good grades or to impress people.* I will try hard to achieve mastery, without worrying about how I compare with others.

- *I believe in myself and in my ability to succeed.* I will have problems and make mistakes, but I will solve those problems and learn from my mistakes.

Chapter 5 will suggest some specific ways to develop these attitudes; it will also identify the motivation skills that students need.

CONCLUDING NOTE

Presenting this detailed portrait of an effective classroom is not suggesting that every class must be like this or implying that you should leave the profession if you can't consistently achieve these goals. It is instead a vision that you can hold for yourself as you think about improving your teaching. Like all visions, it is never fully realized, but it keeps your energies focused on what really matters. If all teachers could develop classrooms that came close to this vision, then all other reform initiatives would be unnecessary.

FOR FURTHER READING

Good, T.L. and Brophy, J.E. 1987. *Looking in classrooms.* 4th ed. New York: Harper & Row. A very useful resource for learning about and using research to improve your own teaching.

31

Rosenholtz, S.J. 1989. *Teachers' workplace: The social organization of schools.* New York: Longman. An excellent description of the school as a workplace and its implications for the classroom.

REFERENCES

Ames, R.E. and Ames, C. 1984. *Research on student motivation: Student motivation,* vol. 1. New York: Academic Press.

Applebee, A.N. 1986. Problems in process approaches: Toward a reconceptualization of process instruction. In *The teaching of writing,* eds. A.S. Petrosky and D. Bartholomae, 95-113. Chicago: University of Chicago Press.

Brophy, J.E. and Alleman, J. 1991. A caveat: Curriculum integration isn't always a good idea. *Educational Leadership* 49(2): 66.

Brophy, J.E. and Good, T.L. 1986. Teacher behavior and student achievement. In *Handbook of research on teaching,* ed. M.C. Wittrock, 3rd ed., 328–75. New York: Macmillan.

Dyson, A.H. and Freedman, S.W. 1991. Writing. In *Handbook of research on teaching the English language arts,* eds. J. Flood, J.M. Jensen, D. Lapp, and J.R. Squire; 754–74. New York: Macmillan.

Glatthorn, A.A. 1990. *Supervisory leadership.* New York: Harper-Collins.

Good, T.L. and Brophy, J.E. 1987. *Looking in classrooms.* 4th ed. New York: Harper & Row.

Hillocks, G., Jr. 1986. *Research on written composition.* Urbana, Ill.: National Conference on Research in English.

Holly, W.J. 1987. *Student self-esteem and academic success.* Eugene, Ore.: Oregon School Study Council, University of Oregon.

Joyce, B. and Weil, M. 1986. *Models of teaching*. 3rd ed. Englewood Cliffs, N.J.: Prentice-Hall.

Chapter 3

AN INTERACTIVE CURRICULUM DEVELOPMENT PROCESS

Chapter 2 mentioned that one key ingredient of effective classrooms is a meaningful curriculum. This chapter explains some basic concepts and interactive processes that you and your colleagues can use in developing that curriculum.

THE BASIC CONCEPTS

There are two important ways to think of curriculum—according to its sources and according to its nature.

The Sources of the Curriculum

First, there are eight types of curriculum that can be identified by their sources (Figure 3-1).

The *hidden curriculum* is what your school teaches day by day through its culture and its climate, its rules and its norms. It is the unintended curriculum that impacts upon the student in subtle but crucial ways. Here are some key components of the hidden curriculum: the policies that allocate power, authority, and resources; the rules that govern the behavior of administrators, teachers, and students; the physical appearance of the building; the punishment and reward system; the relationships between administrators, teachers, and students.

The *recommended curriculum* is the curriculum that professional organizations, prestigious commissions, and assorted experts believe the schools should teach. The recommended curriculum usually appears in books, monographs, and journal articles. The widely publicized *Curriculum and Evaluation Standards* of the National Council of Teachers of Mathematics (NCTM 1989) is one of the best examples of a recommended curriculum.

35

Figure 3-1
CURRICULA ANALYZED IN RELATION TO SOURCES

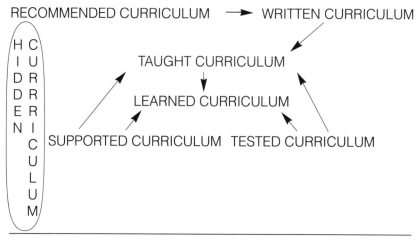

(EXCLUDED CURRICULUM)

The *written curriculum* represents the curriculum documents produced by the state and the local school district. It is the curriculum embodied in the guides that chiefly lie unused on the teacher's shelf. Its main purpose is to control what is taught in classrooms, thus standardizing what is learned throughout a given state or district.

The *taught curriculum* is the curriculum you deliver day by day in your classroom; it is the curriculum that you operationalize.

The *learned curriculum* is the bottom-line curriculum—what students actually learn, what they understand and retain from all your teaching.

The *supported curriculum* is the curriculum found in the textbooks, software, and media used by teachers. Its main purpose is to support the written and the taught curriculum.

The *tested curriculum* is the curriculum that is assessed by standardized tests, end-of-course tests, and classroom tests.

The *excluded curriculum* is the curriculum that has been left out of all the above. A high school social studies teacher can teach in a standard U. S. history course only a fraction of what historians know. Because of the impact of the seven other curricula, the teacher probably leaves out or excludes such topics as the influence of religion in America's past, the importance of labor unions, the contributions of the working class, and the interaction of the arts and the society.

How do these several curricula interact? The research presents the following general picture (Glatthorn 1987):

First, the hidden curriculum has a significant influence on the students; day by day they are learning unintended lessons about what counts and what does not matter in their school and in the larger society.

Next, the recommended curriculum (with the exception of the NCTM *Curriculum and Evaluation Standards*) has little impact on the written and the taught. Curriculum supervisors and classroom teachers typically view these recommendations as too idealistic and too insensitive to the realities of the classroom.

The written curriculum has only a modest influence on the taught curriculum; teachers refer to the curriculum guide only occasionally for general guidance.

The supported curriculum seems to vary in its impact; elementary teachers who are required to teach several subjects probably rely more upon the textbook than do secondary teachers.

The tested curriculum seems to be having a major impact on the taught and the learned curriculum. The increasing use of state-mandated and district-imposed tests constrains what teachers teach. Wisely, they reason that if they are to be held accountable for test results, then they had better emphasize test content. Almost all teachers do so in a professionally honest manner, focusing on test content without teaching test items.

As you probably are aware, there is a major gap between the taught and the learned curriculum. Despite your best efforts, many students are not motivated to learn, have problems learning, and only feign attention. The consequence is diminished achievement.

Finally, the excluded curriculum has an obvious impact that is difficult to measure precisely. Students are taught a curriculum that often seems to represent a homogenized and conservative view of knowledge. They read only literature that literary scholars approve, study history as textbook authors see it, and learn a "scientific method" that is quite unlike the way real scientists reason and discover (Beyer and Apple 1988).

These types of curricula and their relative influence have clear implications for you and your colleagues. As will be explained more fully later in this chapter, you can analyze and modify the hidden curriculum, you can influence the written curriculum (taking cognizance of the recommended), you can energize the taught curriculum, and you can strengthen the connections between the taught and the learned.

The Nature of Curriculum

The curriculum can be analyzed also in relation to its nature. Three types of curricula can be identified here, each with a very different nature. Figure 3-2 shows schematically how they relate.

Figure 3-2
TYPES OF CURRICULUM

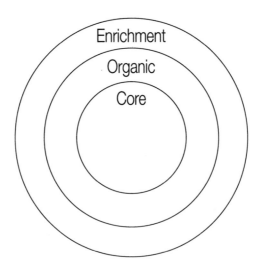

Enrichment
Organic
Core

The *core curriculum* is that curriculum that meets two criteria. First, it encompasses the concepts and skills necessary for *all* students to master. The word *all* represents every student in the school, regardless of ability or so-called "handicapping condition." (The intention is to provide a high quality curriculum for all students.) Second, it is best learned with a high degree of structure or organization; it should not be left to chance. Here are some characteristics of the essential, high-structure core:

- It should focus on the essential skills and knowledge that all students should master.
- It should relate directly to the goals or outcomes of K–12 education.
- It should be carefully sequenced from grade to grade.
- It should be specified with clear objectives.
- It should be planned for and organized into well-structured units and lessons.
- It should be supported with high quality materials.
- It should be carefully assessed.
- It should be embodied in a carefully planned set of documents and stored into a computer bank for easy retrieval.

The *organic curriculum* is just as important as the core; however, it does not require the high structure of the core. The term *organic* connotes its key attributes; it is nurtured and cultivated rather than taught. Consider, for example, this objective: *The student will enjoy reading poetry.*

That is an organic outcome. If you are an English language arts teacher, you foster enjoyment every time you teach a poem. It is not a third grade objective; it is an everyday objective. Most of the affective outcomes are better treated as organic outcomes; they are best nurtured every day, rather than being allocated to a specific grade or a particular unit.

Here are some more organic outcomes:

39

- Develop scientific curiosity.
- Respect those from other cultures.
- Value mathematics as a way of knowing.
- Cooperate effectively with other students.

The *enrichment curriculum* is the optional part of the curriculum; it is not essential for all students. However, rather than providing the enrichment curriculum only for the gifted, the model I have developed provides enrichment for all students. You and your colleagues collaboratively plan units that tap your special knowledge and interests and respond to the particular needs of your students.

This analysis has some critical implications for you and your colleagues as they relate to how time is used and how the curriculum is developed. Consider the following recommendations:

1. The core curriculum should require from 25–75 per cent of available classroom time; the specific amount should be determined by age of students and the complexity of the subject. The core curriculum should be standardized throughout the school district, so that all students have access to a high quality curriculum; what they learn is not dependent upon which school they attend or to which group they are assigned. The core curriculum should be developed by a district-wide committee, with considerable input from the classroom teachers. And it should be formalized into teacher-friendly curriculum guides and stored in a computer bank for easy retrieval.

2. The organic curriculum should require from 15–50 per cent of the time; again, the specific percentage would depend upon the students and the subject. While it should be clearly delineated, it does not require scope-and-sequence charts or curriculum guides. It can be best implemented through effective staff development. The same district-wide committee that developed the core should also delineate the organic

curriculum, again with input from the teachers. Figure 3-3 provides an example of the organic curriculum for English language arts.

Figure 3-3
ORGANIC OUTCOMES FOR ENGLISH
LANGUAGE ARTS

The following outcomes should be emphasized on a continuing basis and nurtured on every appropriate occasion.

- Enjoy reading all forms of literature.
- Value writing as a way of knowing and communicating.
- Value language as a priceless human heritage.
- Value one's own dialect and accept the dialects of others.
- Listen courteously and attentively.
- Speak clearly and courteously, without bias.
- Cooperate effectively in learning and in solving problems.

3. The enrichment curriculum should require from 10–20 per cent of the time. It should be developed by teams of teachers working together at the school level. It does not need to be standardized throughout the school district.

INTERACTIVE PROCESSES FOR CURRICULUM DEVELOPMENT

There are obviously many ways that you and your colleagues can influence curriculum development. The processes described below seem to be the most important ones you should use.

Analyze and Modify the Hidden Curriculum

You and the rest of the faculty should enlist the active support of the principal in analyzing and modifying your school's hidden curriculum.

There are several approaches to analyzing the hidden curriculum. The one that follows has been used by several school faculties to assess the hidden curriculum of their school.

Clarify Your Values

Before you analyze the hidden curriculum and the values it might be transmitting, you should understand the values that matter to you and your colleagues. You can begin this process by generating your own tentative list of the values you believe in, or, you may wish to use the list shown in Figure 3-4. The values delineated there have been drawn from an analysis of three sources: the values of our democratic society, the research on effective schools, and the research on effective business organizations. Regardless of whether you generate your own or use the one shown here, you and your colleagues need to have some open dialogue about the values that count.

As a result of that discussion, you and your colleagues should then be able to produce a clear statement of the faculty's values, which can be presented to several constituencies as the faculty philosophy.

The next step would be to involve the parents in similar discussions, as a means of building consensus. The results of the parent discussions can then be reviewed by the faculty and incorporated in a revised version of the philosophy.

Finally, the students should be involved in thinking about the values. Primary grade teachers may have to simplify the statements so that they are understandable by younger children. The statement for democracy (Figure 3-4) might be modified this way:

> Everyone has a say in what happens, even if he or she is not grown up. Grownups have more of a say because they know more. If you are affected by a decision, you have a chance to tell what you think should be done.

Assess Perceptions of the Existing Hidden Curriculum

With those values clarified and made explicit, you and

Figure 3-4
THE VALUES OF OUR SCHOOL

1. DEMOCRACY. Power is shared with all those involved, within the limits of each person's maturity. In other words, all those affected by decisions have a voice in making those decisions.
2. JUSTICE. People are treated equally–regardless of race, gender, social class, or status. No favoritism is shown to anyone; no individual or group is stigmatized. Fairness and due process are accorded to all.
3. HUMAN DIVERSITY. People are valued for their individual contributions. All human talents are recognized and rewarded. All cultures represented in the school are valued and given due recognition.
4. CLIENT ORIENTATION. All decisions are made and resources used according to the client's needs. In the case of schools, the school is student-oriented; student work is valued and respected.
5. EXCELLENCE. There is a general regard for excellence in performance and output. High standards and expectations are held for all in the organization.
6. COLLEGIALITY. Administrators, teachers, students, and parents work together collaboratively to achieve the goals of the organization. A spirit of cooperation pervades the classroom, the school organization, and home-school relationships.
7. PURPOSEFULNESS. The school has a clear and continuing focus on learning outcomes. The organization's goals are clearly articulated, understood, and accepted by all. Everyone in the school has a sense of purpose and is motivated to achieve that purpose.
8. OPENNESS. Honesty and openness are valued. All decisions are made in an open manner. Feedback is constructive and is welcomed as a key ingredient of improvement.
9. IMPROVEMENT ORIENTATION. The organization is concerned with improvement. Experimenting and trying new approaches are encouraged. Failure is seen as an opportunity for growth; risk-taking is encouraged.
10. AESTHETIC AND ENVIRONMENTAL AWARENESS. Resources are used efficiently; waste is discouraged. The school observes sound principles of environmental awareness. All learning and work spaces are attractive.

your colleagues are now ready to turn your attention to the assessment of the hidden curriculum as it currently exists.

To do this, you should begin with a survey of faculty perceptions. The survey presented in Figure 3-5 was developed in a very systematic way. First, the elements of the hidden curriculum (such as 'decision making') were identified by reviewing the literature on school climate, school culture, and the hidden curriculum. Then the core values that had been identified were analyzed as they related to and impacted upon those elements, and their interaction was analyzed into the series of statements shown in the figure. Each value is reflected in at least two of the operative statements. Thus, the value of democracy when manifested in the decision-making process yields a behavior: "Decisions are made with appropriate input from all those affected and involved."

The scoring of the instrument is rather simple, especially if you use computer-scannable response sheets. By assigning values to each response (4 to "strongly agree," 3 to "agree" 2 to "disagree," and 1 to "strongly disagree"), you can easily compute means for each item. Although the survey instrument has not been validated for research purposes, it has been used effectively by several faculties.

When the results of the faculty surveys have been analyzed, you should then decide what additional input you need. (You may even decide that you wish to get input from students and parents.)

Modifying Discrepant Elements

The final step in the process is to review the results with the rest of the faculty and develop a plan of action. You and the school administrators should examine closely those categories and individual items that have the lowest scores to determine the focus of your work. In deciding how many areas or items you wish to work on, you should also consider the resources available and your other school-improvement priorities.

Figure 3-5
ASSESSING THE HIDDEN CURRICULUM

Your responses to the following survey will help us assess our school's *hidden curriculum*. The hidden curriculum is the set of values, norms, and practices that teach students unintended lessons. Read each statement about the hidden curriculum. In the blank next to each statement, tell us to what extent that statement is true of our school. Use the following code:

4: To a great extent
3: To a moderate extent
2: To less extent
1: To no extent at all

THE PHYSICAL ENVIRONMENT

_____ 1. The school is clean, attractive, and well maintained.
_____ 2. The school does not waste materials and operates in an environmentally sensitive manner.
_____ 3. Everyone cooperates in developing and maintaining an appropriate environment for learning.
_____ 4. Student work is displayed throughout the school.

SCHOOL DISCIPLINE

_____ 5. The rules have been developed with appropriate teacher, student, and parent input.
_____ 6. Disciplinary policies are administered consistently and even-handedly, and with a concern for due process.

COMMUNICATION PROCESSES

_____ 7. Written and oral communication is free of gender and ethnic bias.
_____ 8. Announcements are made and messages delivered in a manner that does not intrude on instruction.
_____ 9. Communication within the school and with the home is constructive and respectful; negative messages are delivered in a manner that fosters growth.

DECISION MAKING

_____ 10. Decisions are made with appropriate input from all those affected and involved.

_____ 11. Decisions are made openly, except where confidentiality is required.

_____ 12. Wherever feasible, decisions are made on the basis of a consensus.

RESOURCE ALLOCATION

_____ 13. Resources are allocated on the basis of how they will support the achievement of school goals, not on the status and the power of the recipient.

_____ 14. Resources are allocated through an open process that benefits from the input of all those involved.

REWARD SYSTEM

_____ 15. Academic achievement is given suitable recognition and rewards.

_____ 16. The reward system rewards group accomplishment as well as individual achievement.

_____ 17. The reward system gives appropriate recognition to human talents other than the academic.

_____ 18. The reward system for teachers and students is designed to motivate them to achieve excellence, not simply to meet minimum standards.

PARENT RELATIONSHIPS

_____ 19. Parents are seen as potentially effective partners and resources in the educational enterprise.

_____ 20. Parents are involved in decisions that affect them.

CLASSROOM CLIMATE

_____ 21. The classrooms manifest a spirit of cooperation between teacher and students and between students with each other.

_____ 22. The teacher holds and makes clear high expectations for all learners.

_____ 23. In calling on, responding to, rewarding, and disciplining students, the teacher demonstrates fairness and non-discrimination and creates equal opportunities for all students to learn.

GROUPING

_____ 24. Students are grouped flexibly for instruction, based upon learning needs.
_____ 25. Grouping practices do not stigmatize or stratify the student body.

PROFESSIONAL RELATIONSHIPS

_____ 26. The principal and teachers collaborate in solving school problems.
_____ 27. The teachers work together collaboratively.
_____ 28. The principal and the teachers are improvement-oriented, open to emerging problems, and willing to expend the efforts needed to make improvements.
_____ 29. Teachers are encouraged to take risks and are not criticized for failures that result from such risk-taking.

TIME AND THE SCHOOL SCHEDULE

_____ 30. The schedule is developed with input from teachers.
_____ 31. The schedule is sensitive to students' needs.
_____ 32. The schedule allocates time according to the school's learning priorities.
_____ 33. The schedule is sensitive to the special needs of working parents.

By that process, you will have identified one or more areas or factors that you wish to change. By reflecting about your experiential knowledge and by reviewing the relevant research, you then identify the specific steps that could be taken to improve in that area.

Influence the Written Core Curriculum

Because the written core curriculum should be standardized throughout the school district, you cannot impact upon the core directly. However, you and your colleagues should urge the district leaders to use the following teacher-centered process. (This example assumes that a district has decided to develop a new K–12 core curriculum for science.)

1. Appoint a science-curriculum task force to manage and direct all aspects of the curriculum-development process. Include on the task force representatives from the following groups: central-office science supervisors, school administrators, elementary teachers who are especially skilled in teaching science, middle and high school science teachers.

2. The task force should analyze the recommended curriculum, reviewing the appropriate research and recommendations of experts. Members should organize their findings in a document to be shared with teachers. By analyzing current books written by scientists and reviewing available texts, they should also become aware of the "excluded curriculum," and decide whether parts of it might be included in this project.

3. By analyzing the school district's goals (or exit outcomes) and the recommendations of experts, identify the outcomes for science K–12.

4. Provide staff development to update the knowledge of all classroom teachers who teach science. The staff development should provide teachers with an in-depth knowledge of the

recommended curriculum and the district goals and familiarize them with the curriculum-development process.

5. Survey all teachers who teach science, asking them to identify the core objectives they would like to teach at their grade level or in their subject. Emphasize the following in your survey: you want teachers to recommend objectives for their grade level only; you want them to recommend what they would like to teach, not necessarily what they have taught before; you want them to identify general skills and knowledge, not specific objectives; you want to be sure that the goals of science are achieved.

6. Use the teacher-provided data to develop the first draft of a scope-and-sequence chart.

7. Review the first draft to determine if it appropriately reflects the recommendations of experts, responds to the developmental nature of the learners, provides for sufficient reinforcement without unproductive repetition, and is clearly goal-oriented. Make any necessary modifications.

8. Pay a team of teachers to work over the summer, translating the general scope-and-sequence chart into specific grade-level objectives.

9. Develop a "teacher-friendly" curriculum guide that identifies the subject goals, lists all the core objectives grade by grade, delineates the organic curriculum for all grades, and makes general recommendations for the allocation of time.

10. Develop the tests and other performance measures needed to assess student learning of the core.

Note that the curriculum guide should not specify how teachers should teach the objectives, when they should teach them, or how they should integrate them. These matters should be left to the individual classroom teacher to decide. The goal is to develop a teacher-friendly guide that is easy to use, that clearly specifies the core, and that provides teachers with the professional autonomy they need.

Energize the Taught Curriculum with Problem-Centered Core Units

This next process may well be the most important of all. You and your colleagues should now take that "lean and mean" curriculum guide and energize it by developing problem-centered units. These problem-centered units are constructed so that they reflect the best current knowledge about teaching problem-solving and critical thinking. Here are the essential principles of such an approach:

- Thinking skills are best taught in the context of solving complex problems, not in isolation. Rather than teaching an isolated skill such as "drawing inferences," you help the students solve a complex problem, teaching the skills they need as they need them.

- As much as possible, those problems should be meaningful ones—important in that subject and significant to the student.

- Those problems should require the student to master and use the core knowledge of that subject. Knowledge is essential for problem-solving—but it must become generative knowledge that students use in solving problems, not simply facts to be remembered (Resnick and Klopfer 1989).

Developing high quality problem-centered units is a complex and time-consuming task. If at all possible, you and your teammates should be provided with the staff development and the quality time you need to produce such units. Here is a brief description of one process that seems to work well:

Begin the process by developing a tentative list of all the units you will teach for the year. Review the core-curriculum guide, think about your particular students, and analyze the materials available, such as software and texts. List the titles of the units

50

and the approximate amount of time each unit will require. In making these preliminary decisions, remember that problem-solving units usually require more time than knowledge-coverage units. Also keep in mind that most curriculum experts believe that "less is more"—in-depth knowledge is better than superficial coverage.

With those preliminary decisions made, turn to the process of developing each unit. There are many processes recommended for unit development; the one outlined below seems to work effectively for developing problem-centered units. (The examples used here assume that a team of teachers is developing an eighth-grade unit integrating English language arts and social studies.)

1. *Frame the unit.* For each unit, identify the unit title, the general unit goal or outcome, the central problem to be solved, and the amount of time available. This is how these decisions might look:

UNIT TITLE: Muted Voices

UNIT GOAL OR OUTCOME: Understand how certain groups (typically not represented in textbooks) perceived the period known as "Westward Expansion."

CENTRAL PROBLEM TO SOLVE: How did African-Americans, Native Americans, and women feel about and participate in the actions known as the "Westward Expansion"?

TIME AVAILABLE: 3 weeks

2. *Develop the unit scenario.* The unit scenario is a dynamic sketch of how you see the general learning processes take place over the life of the unit. You consider the unit goal, the central problem, the students and their abilities and interests, and the materials available. You develop an image of how the learning

51

takes place. Here is an example using the unit identified above:

The unit begins by assessing students' present knowledge of the period—knowledge based on standard textbooks, movies, and television shows. Then the whole class gets some basic information about the period as it is usually conceptualized—the dates, the major events, and the key players. We then talk about whose voices are not heard in that standard account. They may need some cuing to identify these groups. They then form small groups—probably one each for African Americans, Native Americans, and women. Each group works in the library to locate sources (need to check with the librarian here) and to get the knowledge it needs. Each group decides how its members will present their findings—speak their voices—possibly through role plays, dramatizations, original newspapers, or reports. We end by discussing the larger issue—the textbook usually represents the voice of the dominant majority, so we need to learn how to listen to the muted voices.

3. *Review the scenario to be sure that it meets certain criteria.* Here are the criteria: the scenario enables students to achieve the unit goal and solve the central problem, it provides the students with the knowledge they need to solve the problem, it makes use of effective and varied teaching and learning strategies, it reflects the developmental abilities and needs of the students, and it provides sufficient time for mastery.

4. *Turn the scenario into a series of structured lessons.* At this stage it usually is helpful to construct a large chart that lists the identifying information (unit title, grade level, subject or subjects, unit goal or outcome, and general problem to be solved), the days of the unit in sequence, the learning objectives, the learning activities, the means of assessment that will be used, and the special resources needed. (See Figure 3-6.)

Figure 3-6
UNIT PLANNING CHART

Unit Title: _____ Grade: _____

Subject(s): _____

Unit Goal(s) or Outcome(s): _____

Problem to Solve: _____

....

                       DAY 1   DAY 2

LEARNING OBJECTIVE

LEARNING ACTIVITIES

GROUP STRUCTURE

ASSESSMENT

RESOURCES NEEDED

This chart is designed to integrate both the unit-planning and the daily planning process. It also helps you work out the details of the scenario, to be sure that its general features can be operationalized in the time available.

5. *Locate and develop necessary materials.* Because the problem-solving units will often require knowledge that is unavailable in standard textbooks, you should devote some special efforts to locating materials already produced—or to developing such materials.

Should all such units be integrated? As you are aware, there is currently much interest in integrated curricula that draw from two or more different subjects. While there is some evidence that integrated units are more effective than single-subject units in developing desired attitudes and that they are just as effective in improving achievement, you should keep in mind the cautions advanced earlier in this book by Brophy and Alleman (1991)—that curriculum integration is a means, not an end; and that if you don't keep this in mind during development, your integrated unit can easily become a poorly designed collection of interesting activities without sufficient structure.

For more information on how to develop integrated units, read R. Fogarty's book, *The Mindful School: How to Integrate the Curricula* (1991).

Develop Enrichment Programs

The next major way you can influence the curriculum is to work with colleagues at your grade level in developing the enrichment units. As explained previously, the enrichment units are designed to reflect your special strengths and interests, to broaden the curriculum beyond the core, and to appeal and respond to the special needs and interests of your students.

You and your team of colleagues should begin the process by making a tentative list of the enrichment units you believe should be available to students. Here are some questions to ask as you think about developing such a list.

1. What is the excluded curriculum and how might it be included?
2. What current issues are surfacing now that were not important when the core was developed?
3. What new knowledge in this subject area is now available that was not known when the core was developed?
4. To what extent does the core curriculum ignore the special contributions of minority groups represented in our school?
5. What special student interests are not reflected in the core?
6. What special teacher knowledge and interests are not reflected in the core?
7. What new materials are available now that could play a central role in the enrichment curriculum?

Each grade-specific team should submit its tentative list to a school-wide curriculum committee for review. By receiving and reviewing lists from all grade levels, the committee can identify such problems as excessive repetition, undesirable controversy, and trivialized learning. Even though most teachers can be trusted to avoid such problems, some type of large-picture review can at times be useful.

When your list has been approved, your team should probably develop the first enrichment unit together, so that it can work out the process and the forms it wishes to use. After that first unit has been developed, you and your colleagues might then decide to work independently.

Strengthen the Connections Between The Taught and the Learned

The final major way you can influence curricula is by strengthening the connections between the taught and the learned through effective teaching. You probably have your own way of accomplishing this task. The following discussion simply calls your attention to some teacher-tested and research-based strategies that seem to work.

First, be sure the students understand the learning objectives for that lesson. While I do not believe in requiring teachers to write the objectives on the board, it is important to ensure clarity of understanding. And you do not have to use "behavioral" language. Here is a satisfactory statement, even though it has some verbal imprecision:

> Class, we're going to find out today how you can interpret the lyrics to a song when they seem to have several possible meanings.

Second, give the students a verbal or diagrammatic map of the lesson to come. They will remember better if they see the big picture and understand how the parts connect. Here is an example:

> So this is what will happen. We'll listen to a tape of a song. We'll read the lyrics. Each of you will write your own interpretation. We'll share the interpretations with each other. Then we'll discuss strategies each of you used to figure out a meaning. The main thing is to work out the strategies, not to argue about specific interpretations.

Next, use cues and signals to indicate what is really important. You can use verbal cues such as these: *here comes a key point, check this main idea, write this strategy in your brain.* Also make judicious use of the chalkboard. Students pay attention to what you write on the board. Some teachers make the mistake of cluttering up the board with trivia.

Periodically assess learning. Monitor student attention; watch for nonverbal signs of confusion or uncertainty. Ask questions of nonvolunteers to check for understanding.

Use writing to reinforce learning. From time to time, ask students to write in their notebooks their own understanding of a concept. Make this an active learning process by requiring them to use their own words, instead of copying yours. Obviously, you should check such work. Finally, save time at the end of class to pull things together. It is good practice to ask students to summarize, rather than summarize the lesson yourself.

CONCLUDING NOTE

All the above work will obviously require some special training and quality time. And not all teachers will want to be involved. However, the curriculum is one of the most important elements in the educational process. You and your colleagues should play a key role in its development.

FOR FURTHER READING

Connelly, E.M. and Clandinin, D.J. 1988. *Teachers as curriculum planners: Narratives of experience.* New York: Teachers College Press. A highly original work that takes a different approach to teacher involvement in the curriculum process—one that emphasizes the importance of teachers' personal, practical knowledge.

Glatthorn, A.A. 1987. *Curriculum renewal.* Alexandria, Vir.: Association for Supervision and Curriculum Development. A "nuts and bolts" manual on how to develop curricula.

McCarthy, B. 1980. *The 4MAT system.* Oak Brook, Ill.: EXCEL. A practical model for developing curricula that respond to learning style differences.

REFERENCES

Beyer, L.E. and Apple, M.W. 1988. *The curriculum: Problems, politics, and possibilities.* Albany, N.Y.: State University of New York Press.

Brophy, J. and Alleman, J. 1991. A caveat: Curriculum integration isn't always a good idea. *Educational Leadership,* 49(2): 66.

Fogarty, R. 1991. *The mindful school: How to integrate the curricula.* Palatine, Ill.: Skylight.

Glatthorn, A.A. 1987. *Curriculum leadership.* New York: HarperCollins.

National Council of Teachers of Mathematics (NCTM). 1989. *Curriculum and evaluation standards for school mathematics.* Reston, Vir.: NCTM.

Resnick, L.B. and Klopfer, L.E. (eds.) 1989. *Toward the thinking curriculum: Current cognitive research.* Alexandria, Vir.: Association for Supervision and Curriculum Development.

Chapter 4

PROFESSIONAL DEVELOPMENT PROGRAMS

You have been to many inservice meetings where some star of the consultant circuit brought you the latest word about learning styles (or some other "hot" topic) and then departed, leaving you with questions unanswered and needs unmet. And you probably have been supervised by a principal who visited your classroom twice last year and then conducted a "good news/bad news" conference that told you what you already knew about your teaching. Those ineffective processes need to be abandoned.

In their place you and your colleagues need professional programs and processes that reflect what is known about teachers' development, that respect the professionalism of teachers, and that integrate teachers' personal growth and school-improvement measures. That is what this chapter is all about. It first describes how the school as an organization can support the professional sdevelopment of the staff. It then presents a current model of teacher development that respects the individuality of teachers. The chapter concludes by explaining how you and your colleagues can plan and implement inservice programs with real power.

THE ORGANIZATIONAL CONTEXT

Your growth as a teacher does not take place in a vacuum; it is directly affected by the nature of the organization of which you are a part. Figure 4-1 lists the key features of an organizational environment that supports the professional development of the faculty.

There are several ways you and your colleagues can use this list of key factors. First, you should review it, discuss it, and

Figure 4-1

ORGANIZATIONAL FACTORS SUPPORTING TEACHERS' PROFESSIONAL DEVELOPMENT

THE ORGANIZATIONAL STRUCTURE

1. The principal and the teachers hold a set of beliefs on facilitating professional development—beliefs that value collegiality and cooperation, experimentation and improvement, and high expectations for all.
2. The principal and the teachers support and work toward achieving a common set of goals.

THE FORMAL AND INFORMAL ORGANIZATION

3. The formal organization is characterized by an optimal balance between tight and loose structure and between principal leadership and teacher power; teachers have sufficient autonomy within the limits of the school's and district's need for coordination.
4. The informal organization supports the professional norms related to the values articulated above; there is a strong sense of staff cohesiveness, with positive relationships between administrators and teachers.

THE ROLE OF THE TEACHER

5. Teachers receive increased autonomy in the areas of curriculum, instruction, and their own professional development.
6. Teaching is perceived by all as a highly skilled and very demanding profession.

TEACHERS' UNIONS

7. The teachers' union supports the professional development of teachers and avoids excessive standardization of the profession.

PRINCIPAL AND PEER RELATIONSHIPS

8. The principal works with teachers in developing and sustaining an organizational environment that reflects both this general research and the special needs of that context.

9. Teachers believe in and practice collegiality; they learn from and with each other by observing, conferring, coaching, researching, and producing materials; they collaborate to achieve joint goals.

ORGANIZATIONAL SUPPORT SYSTEM

10. Teachers are provided with an orderly, clean, and safe physical environment, are given sufficient time to plan and teach effectively, are provided quality time for their own growth, and are provided with the needed fiscal resources.
11. Teachers are rewarded for growth, risk-taking, and change; reward systems reinforce collegiality, not competitiveness.

SOURCES: Corcoran 1990, Flinders 1989, Johnson and Johnson 1989, McLaughlin and Yee 1988.

revise it, adding to the empirical research your own experiential knowledge of a growth-enhancing environment. Second, with your principal's cooperation, you can use that revised list to survey faculty members about their perceptions of your school's environment. Finally, you and your colleagues can work with your principal to modify those aspects of the environment that, according to the evaluation, need improvement.

A DIFFERENTIATED MODEL OF PROFESSIONAL DEVELOPMENT

A supportive context is helpful but not sufficient for faculty growth. You and your colleagues also need a home-grown model for professional development that takes cognizance of the fact that teachers differ in their developmental needs and preferences. The problem with the standard models of clinical supervision is that they provide the same services to uncertain beginners and experienced experts: everyone gets two observations and conferences that focus on the basic skills of teaching. For the past 10 years, I have been helping local school systems develop and implement a model that respects teachers' differing needs and preferences. It is presented here as a set of guidelines that you and your colleagues can use in developing your own model.

1. *Distinguish between evaluation and development.* There is a fundamental difference between the processes needed to evaluate teachers and those needed to facilitate their growth. Too many school districts confuse and intermingle these processes. They should be kept separate.

   First, every school system needs a rigorous teacher evaluation system that ensures that incompetent teachers who do not demonstrate the capacity for growth are professionally terminated. These evaluation systems should be used with all nontenured teachers and for any tenured teacher who, in

62

retrospect, should not have been granted tenure. That group of individuals probably constitutes no more than 10 percent of the faculty. All the rest of the faculty should be evaluated only for improvement purposes, and only once every four or five years. As Glickman (1991) notes, evaluation does not improve instruction, despite the assertions of numerous educators. (Turn to Chapter 8 for further discussion of the teacher evaluation system.)

Second, every school system needs a supportive professional development system that is designed solely to foster growth, not to evaluate. (The discussion that follows will help you develop such a system.)

2. *Establish a professional development committee.* If you do not have a standing committee concerned with teacher development, you and your colleagues should establish one. Its membership should include the following: a central office supervisor, the school principal or assistant principal, a team leader or department chair, and one or more classroom teachers. The committee should develop, implement, and monitor the model it thinks will work best in your school. The committee, of course, should work closely with district leaders, to be sure that school plans are coordinated with district efforts.

3. *Provide intensive development for those who need special help.* The term *intensive development* is used here to describe a highly concentrated form of what is usually called "clinical supervision." In its best form, an expert mentor works with a novice (or an experienced teacher who needs help) in a close and supportive relationship. There is no evaluation; the entire thrust is developmental. The mentor observes, confers, coaches, shares materials, gives advice, listens supportively, and acts as an advocate.

This intensive development is a time-consuming process, one that typically requires at least 20 hours for each mentoring relationship if it is to be effective. However, such intensive assistance by a mentor pays off, as several research studies indicate (Huling-Austin 1990).

For maximum effectiveness, such mentoring programs should observe the following research-based guidelines.

- The mentoring program should be flexible, responding to the changing needs of the teacher involved.
- The program should make only reasonable demands on the mentor's time and it should not impose unnecessary burdens upon the teacher who needs mentoring.
- The program should emphasize reflection and decision-making, but should also ensure that the teacher has mastered the basic skills.
- The program should be developmental, not evaluative; all information developed in the mentoring process should remain confidential, unless the teacher wants to share it with the principal.
- The mentors should be selected carefully and trained effectively (Huling-Austin 1988).

4. *Emphasize cooperative development.* All teachers should be encouraged (but not required) to participate in *cooperative development,* a process by which teams of teachers work together for their professional growth. The cooperative teams should be small (from 3–7 members), should develop a common vocabulary to discuss curriculum and instruction, and, if possible, should share a common set of beliefs about education. The cooperative teams can be structured around an existing team structure (such as a grade-level team or a department) or can be organized on the basis of teachers' expressed preferences for the colleagues with whom they would like to work.

Each team should identify one school-improvement goal that it wishes to focus on, either selecting that goal from the school's improvement plan or by identifying such a goal from team members' own evaluations. Here, for example, is a goal members might select: *Students will improve their thinking skills.*

Observe that the goal is stated in terms of what students will achieve. The team members then determine how they will work together to achieve that goal, and in the process, facilitate their own growth. Here are some of the processes they can use to achieve the goal.

- Professional dialogues. The team members read research reports and articles about the goal, discuss those readings with each other, and synthesize their learning in a written synopsis.
- Materials development. Team members work together to develop the teaching/learning materials required for accomplishing that goal. They use these materials in their own classrooms, revising them on the basis of pilot-test results.
- Peer observation and conferring. Team members observe each other teaching a lesson relating to that goal and give each other feedback. The feedback is supportive and descriptive, not evaluative. If additional training seems needed, the team members include peer coaching as part of this process.
- Action research. Team members plan and implement an action-research project designed to achieve the goal they identified. They identify the problem, gather research related to it, develop a tentative solution to the problem, and implement and evaluate that solution.

Members of a team should systematize their cooperative development plans, have them reviewed by a professional development committee, and revise them as needed. This cooperative development takes the place of the usual clinical supervision for all teachers, except for those who are also involved in the intensive mode.

This very strong recommendation for cooperative development should not be interpreted to mean that it is easy to implement. Many educators note problems with this mode of development: it requires a supportive environment; it requires an openness on the part of its members; it takes time; and it requires teachers to develop new skills (Flinders 1989).

However, you should be assured that the research suggests very strongly that such efforts will pay off for you, your colleagues, and your students.

5. *Provide self-directed development for those who do not wish to participate in the cooperative mode.* While cooperative development is a very effective means for fostering growth, there always will be some teachers who want to work on their own. They may not have the time to work closely with colleagues, or they may not be able to find a team of compatible colleagues. As Flinders (1989) notes, many teachers actually prefer professional isolation to collaboration for two reasons: the isolation gives them a chance to escape the demands of interaction with others and the isolation saves time, a precious commodity for teachers. As a consequence, it seems desirable to provide teachers with a self-directed option that enables them to direct their own growth.

Teachers in a self-directed model would also begin by identifying one school-improvement goal toward which they wish to work, in the process fostering their individual growth. They next should identify what methods they will use to accomplish that goal and how they will demonstrate their accomplishment. Those plans should also be reviewed by a professional development committee, to be sure they are feasible and likely to be effective. (Further details about such a self-directed model can be found in McGreal 1983.)

There are some problems associated with this mode as well. First, many teachers treat the goal-setting process as a

Figure 4-2
RESEARCH FINDINGS ON EFFECTIVE
STAFF DEVELOPMENT

LEADERSHIP

1. School principals and team leaders play an active role in staff-development programs, while enabling teacher-participants to have a significant role in making decisions about the program's content and structure.

RELATIONSHIP TO THE SCHOOL, ITS ENVIRONMENT, AND ITS CULTURE

2. Effective staff development takes place in an organizational environment that supports professional growth; in turn, the staff-development programs are designed to strengthen that environment and build that culture.
3. School-based staff-development programs that are sensitive to the classroom context and the special needs of teachers are in general more effective than district-level staff development that is far removed from the classroom context.

RELATIONSHIP TO SCHOOL IMPROVEMENT AND NEW PROGRAMS

4. Staff development that focuses on planned change is more effective when it responds to teachers' stages of concern about that change.
5. Staff-development programs that provide concrete assistance with the demands of a new program and that help teachers solve problems involved with the new program seem to be effective in sustaining change.

CONTENT AND FOCUS OF STAFF DEVELOPMENT

6. Staff-development programs are more effective when they emphasize the development of reflective inquiry into practice; those that focus on narrow and specific skills seem to have only a short-term effect.
7. Effective staff-development programs focus on increasing teachers' sense of efficacy, by promoting collegial encourage-

ment, giving timely assistance, and assuring teachers of their power in affecting change.

8. Effective staff-development programs emphasize the importance of content knowledge and help teachers develop their content knowledge.

9. Effective staff development takes into account the complexities of classroom life, the demands of teaching, and the burdens imposed by any programmatic change; it reflects the belief that concepts of effective teaching are embedded in particular classroom contexts. As a consequence, these programs help teachers translate general knowledge into context-specific practices.

10. Effective staff-development programs emphasize the importance of and provide support for collegial and collaborative relationships.

SOURCES: Fullan 1990, Lieberman and Miller 1991, McLaughlin 1991.

trivial game, developing meaningless goals just to satisfy administrators' demands. Second, it can reinforce the isolation of teachers. Growth requires feedback—and the self-directed component runs the risk of excluding that feedback.

The differentiated model is not presented as a problem-free panacea; the problems noted above are significant ones that need to be addressed. However, the differentiated model has several tested advantages over the standard clinical model. It gives teachers a choice. It recognizes that teachers differ in their developmental needs. It empowers teachers to take charge of their own growth. It focuses on school improvement, not on narrow skill development.

6. *Provide effective development programs for all teachers.* All these growth processes should be supported with effective staff development or inservice programs. The characteristics of such effective programs are listed in Figure 4-2.

As you review this list of effective characteristics, observe how it differs from much of the staff development typically offered teachers. It emphasizes collaborative leadership in program design and implementation, rather than focusing on the principal's role alone. It is school- and classroom-based, rather than being developed by those far removed from school goals and teachers' needs.

It is closely tied to the school-improvement plan and teachers' concerns about innovations, rather than being presented as an unrelated series of skill-development sessions that ignores teachers' concerns. Program developers analyze the demands of school-improvement interventions and ensure that staff-development sessions give teachers the assistance they need. Those developing the program are aware that teachers' concerns about an innovation move through several stages—and they plan programs accordingly. When a new program is introduced, teachers are first concerned with getting information about the program and understanding how it will impact upon them personally. As the change is implemented, they become more concerned with managing the change; then they become concerned about its impact on students. In later stages they are more interested in collaborating with other teachers relative to the new program and then in internalizing and modifying the innovation (Loucks-Horsley and Stiegelbauer 1991).

Rather than focusing narrowly on specific teaching skills (such as "asking higher order questions"), effective programs nurture in teachers the capacity to become reflective practitioners.

Effective programs also help teachers develop their content knowledge, since a growing body of research indicates that teachers' knowledge is just as important as teachers' skills (Stodolsky 1988).

Finally, these programs, in their structure and content, support the norms of collegiality and cooperation that are so crucial for school effectiveness. Teachers collaborate in planning the sessions, in conducting them, and in applying in their classrooms the skills and knowledge they have learned.

CONCLUDING NOTE

Obviously, all these processes require the joint efforts of district administrators, school administrators, and teachers. You cannot do it alone. However, developing a more professional model for teacher growth may be one of the most important tasks that you and your colleagues can undertake.

FOR FURTHER READING

Lieberman, A., ed. 1990. *Schools as collaborative cultures.* New York: Falmer. Provides a broad and insightful perspective on how schools can develop and support a culture of collaboration.

Loucks-Horsley, S.; Harding, C.K.; Arbuckle, M.A.; Murray, L.B.; Dubea, C.; and Williams, M.K. 1987. *Continuing to learn: A guidebook for teacher development.* Andover, Mass.: Regional Laboratory for Educational Improvement of the Northeast and the Islands. One of the best sources of information about new approaches to teacher development.

Smith, S.C. and Scott, J.J. 1990. *The collaborative school.* Eugene, Ore.: ERIC Clearinghouse on Educational Management, University of Oregon. Examines in a very constructive manner the work-environment needed for effective instruction.

REFERENCES

Corcoran, T.B. 1990. Schoolwork: Perspectives on workplace reform. In *The contexts of teaching in secondary schools: Teachers' realities,* eds. M.W. McLaughlin, J.E. Talbert, and N. Bascia; 142–66. New York: Teachers College Press.

Flinders, D.J. 1989. *Voices from the classroom.* Eugene, Ore.: ERIC Clearinghouse on Educational Management, University of Oregon.

Fullan, M.G. 1990. Change processes in secondary schools: Toward a more fundamental agenda. In *The contexts of teaching in secondary schools: Teachers' realities,* eds. M.W. McLaughlin, J.E. Talbert; and N. Bascia; 224–55. New York: Teachers College Press.

Glickman, C. 1991. Pretending not to know what we know. *Educational Leadership,* 48(8): 4–10.

Huling-Austin, L. 1988. A synthesis of the research on teacher induction programs and practices. Paper presented at annual meeting of the American Educational Research Association, New Orleans.

_____ . 1990. Teacher induction programs and internships. In *Handbook of research on teacher education,* ed. W.R. Houston, 535–48. New York: Macmillan.

Johnson, D.W. and Johnson, R.T. 1989. *Leading the cooperative school.* Edina, Minn.: Interaction Book.

Lieberman, A. and Miller, L. 1991. Revisiting the social realities of teaching. In *Staff development for education in the 90s,* eds. A. Lieberman and L. Miller, 2d ed., 92–112. New York: Teachers College Press.

Loucks-Horsley, S. and Stiegelbauer, S. 1991. Using knowledge of change to guide staff development. In *Staff development for education in the 90s,* eds. A. Lieberman and L. Miller, 2d ed., 15–36. New York: Teachers College Press.

McGreal, T.L. 1983. *Successful teacher evaluation.* Alexandria, Vir.: Association for Supervision and Curriculum Development.

McLaughlin, M.W. 1991. Enabling professional development: What have we learned? In *Staff development for education in the 90s,* eds. A. Lieberman and L. Miller, 2d ed., 61–82. New York: Teachers College Press.

McLaughlin, M.W. and Yee, S.M. 1988. Schools as a place to have a career. In *Building a professional culture in schools,* ed. A. Lieberman, 23–44. New York: Teachers College.

Stodolsky, S. 1988. *The subject matters.* Chicago: University of Chicago Press.

Chapter 5

STUDENT MOTIVATION PROGRAMS

Motivation to learn, as two scholars define it, is the student's tendency to find academic activities meaningful and worthwhile and to make the necessary effort to achieve the benefits of those activities (Good and Brophy, 1987). You may also think of it as an inner drive to achieve in school. In either sense, you obviously cannot motivate students. You can only create the conditions that are likely to increase that drive.

Teachers have always understood the importance of motivation to learn. They know that teaching students with low levels of motivation is frustrating and complicated. They have learned that unmotivated students require continuous pressure and close monitoring during the learning process. Often they have turned to packaged "motivation" programs that promise simple answers. While there are no simple answers, there are specific strategies that you can use in your own classroom, and effective programs that teams of teachers can develop together.

WHAT YOU CAN DO IN YOUR CLASSROOM

Four general factors influence student motivation to learn: you, the teacher; the classroom environment; the learning experience; and the student.

Start with Yourself

You need to develop four key attitudes that will in turn have a positive effect on students: a belief in your own efficacy, a focus on learning, a readiness to share control, and reasonably high expectations for students.

Belief in Your Own Efficacy

A belief in your own efficacy is faith in your ability to

make a difference with your students. Researchers have discovered that teachers with a strong sense of efficacy have a powerful impact on student achievement. They support students and tolerate student challenge. They create a supportive learning environment and encourage student enthusiasm. They create in their classrooms a contagious sense of excitement (Ashton 1985).

Several factors make it difficult for many teachers to develop this sense of efficacy. Low salaries, public criticism, limited collegial interaction, lack of positive feedback from administrators, and the teacher's relative powerlessness within the organization structure all make it difficult for many teachers to develop this sense of power. All teachers are aware of these constraints.

But the best teachers are not overcome by them. They decide that they can and will make a difference, despite all these obstacles. The belief in their own power becomes a self-fulfilling prophecy. They believe they can make a difference. They exert the effort to do so. They observe the impact of specific strategies. They modify techniques that seem less effective.

Focus on Learning

One of the major challenges of teaching is balancing the conflicting roles of teacher and friend. While effective teachers understand the importance of providing emotional support to students when needed, they also realize that their primary role is an instructional one.

Such a focus on the instructional aspects of the teacher's role tends to increase student motivation to learn: the teacher's emphasis on learning sends a message to students that the central business of the classroom is learning, not socializing. As Brophy (1985) discovered, teachers more concerned with their social than their instructional interactions with students seemed at times less effective in dealing with students, were ineffective in working with underachievers, and were less sensitive to achievement-related problems.

Readiness to Share Control

Students feel more motivated in classrooms where they feel they have some measure of control. Students who feel like passive victims who have no choice are not inclined to put forth the effort needed to achieve. Obviously, therefore, you should be ready to give students some choices within limits. Depending on the students' maturity, you can provide options about such matters as the learning strategy to be used and the means by which learning will be assessed.

Teachers, in turn, are affected by the extent to which they are monitored by administrators. A team of researchers concluded that teachers whose performance is closely monitored by principals who use externally set performance standards tend to be more controlling than teachers who are not involved with such systems (Ryan, Connell, and Deci 1985).

Reasonably High Expectations for Students

You have undoubtedly heard many exhortations from administrators and consultants about the need to hold high expectations for students. Those admonitions are well grounded both in the empirical research and in teachers' practical experience. You need to believe in the ability of all your students to achieve. Be especially sensitive to how you treat less able students. Seat them close to you, not in the back of the room. Call on them and give them sufficient time to think and respond. Demonstrate your interest in their academic success, and give them meaningful praise. Finally, avoid stereotyping such students with labels like *at risk, unmotivated,* and *disadvantaged.* Respond to each one as an individual with special strengths, needs, and interests.

A few cautions should be noted here about high expectations. Do not set unrealistic expectations that lead only to frustration and failure. And do not expect that high expectations will accomplish miracles. One study concluded that teachers' expectations accounted for only five percent of the difference in student achievement (Brophy 1985). Finally, do not join the chorus of uninformed critics who claim that most teachers hold low expectations for their students. The research in general suggests that teachers' expectations are generally accurate, not grossly off the mark.

Develop a Motivating Classroom Environment

The second general strategy is to plan and implement a motivating classroom environment. The key features of the environment are these: the degree of structure, the physical environment, the organization of learning, and the social relationships in the classroom.

Degree of Structure

A motivating environment is one that, first of all, has the optimal degree of structure. *Structure,* as the term is used here, refers chiefly to two elements: the number of routines and the presentation of classroom rules.

Expert teachers use several routines to simplify classroom life: they have routines for checking roll, handling absence notes, making assignments, collecting papers, and checking homework. If you have too few routines, student motivation suffers because too much time is spent in negotiating trivial matters. If you have too many routines, classroom life becomes too predictable. What constitutes "too few" and "too many" will depend, of course, on the developmental maturity of students and their cognitive complexity. Younger students need more routines. All students with a low level of cognitive complexity seem to require more routines than those who can reason with greater sophistication.

The way the teacher presents classroom rules is also a factor. All classes need rules if the business of learning is to be accomplished. What makes a difference is the way those rules are presented. Here researchers make a sharp distinction between *informational* limits and *controlling* limits (Ryan, Connell, and Deci 1985). Informational limits are more highly motivating. These limits acknowledge the conflict between choice and limits, respect the child's emotional development, and acknowledge the inherent conflict of interest in acceding to limits.

Here is a teacher presenting informational limits:

> Remember that the schedule we worked out calls for your critical paper to be turned in on Monday. Now, I know you have many other things you would rather do this weekend. Writing a critique of that article will be a challenge for all of you. But we need to move ahead into the next unit. So let's talk a bit about how to organize your time this weekend to get the job done.

Controlling limits emphasize control for the sake of control; they are presented as edicts, not reasonable decisions. Here is a teacher making the same assignment with a controlling orientation.

> Turn in the report on Monday. The reason it's due Monday is that I said so. I set the deadlines, you meet them.

Physical Environment

The physical environment has a moderate effect on student motivation, although it does not seem to be a significant factor in student achievement. The research suggests that the following features would be found in a more motivating classroom environment: sufficient space so there is no crowding; little external noise (from air and road traffic, for example); bright, attractive colors; and furniture that is comfortable without encouraging slouching (Glatthorn 1991).

Experienced teachers have also discovered that they can use bulletin boards and chalkboards to good effect. They display student work as models and incentives. They write provocative questions on the board as a way of stimulating thinking. They post news items that are likely to stimulate discussion and investigation.

The Organization of Learning

Two elements seem crucial as they relate to the way in which learning is organized: meaningfulness and uncertainty.

Meaningfulness is an approach that enables the student to find personal meaning in what is learned. Meaningfulness includes several instructional emphases: the teacher makes clear the purpose of the learning, the teacher presents the new learning so that it builds upon and extends what the student already knows, the teacher helps the student make personal connections with the learning, the teacher emphasizes the value of the learning to the student.

Obviously, meaningful learning is more motivating. However, that does not mean that all learning must be presented as immediately useful or relevant. Learning about the political struggles involved in the ratification of the Constitution is not useful or relevant in the sense that the student can apply it to the solution of some personal problem. However, it is meaningful; it helps the student understand the use of power in resolving societal problems.

Uncertainty about learning is the sense that there is no single right answer, that much learning is unpredictable, and that life abounds with paradoxes and contradictions. Here are some ways to develop uncertainty: encourage students to debate controversial issues, encourage students to defend alternative explanations and interpretations, discuss the unanswered questions and unresolved issues in a particular discipline, demonstrate an experiment that gives unexpected results, emphasize the importance of asking questions, and point out the contradictions and paradoxes in a subject.

As Gagne (1985) notes, an optimal degree of uncertainty can increase student motivation; however, too much uncertainty can be counterproductive for highly anxious students.

Social Relationships in the Classroom

Peer norms and student-grouping practices are two critical elements of the social relationships in the classroom.

Peer norms are the standards of behavior established by the students, not the teacher. In too many instances these peer norms inhibit students' motivation to learn, such as when powerful members espouse norms of not completing assignments, resisting the teacher's attempts to establish order, and reducing the intellectual demands of the classroom.

Effective teachers are sensitive to such norms and work quietly but consistently to alter them. They praise judiciously, without embarrassing students who are cooperating. They provide genuine opportunities for peer leaders to exercise positive leadership in the classroom. They know when to be flexible and when not to yield to student pressures.

The way in which students are grouped for learning is also a factor in student motivation. A large body of research supports the careful and thoughtful use of heterogeneous grouping for most students (Slavin 1988). However, there is some research indicating that the presence of high ability students in a classroom decreases the motivation of low ability students (Ames 1984).

One of the best ways to structure classroom groups is to make appropriate use of cooperative learning. Cooperative learning is effective not only for increasing achievement; it also promotes more positive attitudes toward the subject and increases motivation to learn that subject (Johnson, Johnson, Holubec, and Roy 1984).

The Learning Experience

In determining how the learning experience itself can be more motivating, you should keep in mind three aspects: the learning task, the test, and the reward structure.

The Learning Task

The learning task is what you expect students to do in order to learn, such as the following: write a persuasive essay, solve a mathematics problem, or conduct a laboratory experiment. Keep in mind two general considerations here: give students a choice and design a motivating task.

Giving students a choice about aspects of the task gives them a greater sense of control and makes it easier for them to find meaning in the task. However, the research suggests that giving students choice within limits is better than giving them uncontrolled choice. Here are three examples to show the difference:

No choice: Study the role of pioneer women and then present a dramatic sketch illustrating the problems they faced.

Choice within limits: Study the role of pioneer women and then decide how you can best show your classmates the types of problems they faced.

Uncontrolled choice: Study pioneer life and share your results with the class.

Obviously, the extent and nature of the choices you provide will vary with students' developmental maturity.

A motivating task is characterized by several essential elements. First, it involves a meaningful goal that is clearly stated and is linked with a long-term outcome. Second, it has an optimal degree of ambiguity: the outcome is somewhat uncertain and unpredictable. And the task is a concrete one that requires the student to become involved with both the task and the teacher. Here is an example of a goal that has all these characteristics:

Remember that we are studying how our language is changing. As part of that study, let's find out how new words come into the language. We can then make up some new words ourselves. Each group has received a list of new words that have come into the language in the past 20 years. Look up their origins in the dictionary. Then decide what your group's words have in common. When you have finished your investigation, each group will present a brief report on its findings.

The Test

You have to assess learning—and tests are an easy way to do that. However, too much emphasis upon tests can reduce the student's inner drive to learn (Maehr 1984). Emphasize the successful accomplishment of the task to be tested, instead of doing well on the test. And present tests as an opportunity to get feedback about learning.

Also be aware of students with high test anxiety. Such students worry too much about tests, become upset when taking tests, and are obsessively concerned with test results. Give these students full information about the test. Show them sample items and let them practice on such items. And again, emphasize the task, not the test.

The Reward Structure

The rewards you give students can be classified as either extrinsic or intrinsic. Extrinsic rewards are those outside and unrelated to the task itself: prizes, happy faces, and parties. Intrinsic rewards are those that are inherent in the accomplishment of the task: a sense of satisfaction in completing the task, an increase in competence in learning something new, and a growing belief in one's ability to achieve.

Extrinsic rewards have some uses. They tend to increase the effort applied to the task and are thus effective with students who need to make a greater effort. And they seem especially suited to boring and routine tasks where quantity is more important than quality.

However, they also have some severe limitations. They can lead students to set easily attainable goals and avoid challenges. They also make students more rigid in their mental activity. Finally, they distract students from the learning task itself (Good and Brophy 1987).

The research suggests that you should place a greater emphasis on intrinsic rewards, using extrinsic rewards only when the task is routine or with students who need to make greater effort.

Student Factors

Of all the factors that you can influence, perhaps the most significant is the student—his or her attitudes and skills.

Student Attitudes

The attitudes you should attempt to develop in students were listed in Chapter 2. The research indicates quite clearly that students who have those attitudes will have a stronger drive to achieve. The most significant attitudes are discussed briefly below to clarify their meaning and reinforce their importance.

The first crucial attitude involves a success orientation. Highly motivated students focus on achieving success. Less motivated students are concerned with avoiding failure and demonstrate the following behaviors: reluctance to participate, unwillingness to do extra work, unreasonable goal-setting that will provide an excuse for failure, procrastination, and/or selection of very easy tasks. All of these behaviors are self-defeating.

Second, motivated students understand that success results from a combination of ability and effort. When they fail, they attribute the failure to a lack of effort. Less motivated students attribute their success to external factors, such as luck, easiness of the task, or teacher generosity; they attribute failure to a lack of ability (Covington 1984).

Highly motivated students see themselves as origins, not pawns. Students who believe they are origins believe they control and cause their behavior; they believe they have choices and experience a sense of freedom; they accept responsibility for their choices. Those who see themselves as pawns believe they are pushed around by external forces; they believe they have little freedom and do not feel responsible for their actions (deCharms 1984).

A fourth key attitude is a belief that abilities can be developed. Students feel more motivated to learn mathematics when they are convinced that, with the aid of classmates and teachers, they can improve their ability in mathematics. Students who express an attitude of "I'm just dumb when it comes to math" are less motivated to learn.

Finally, motivated students have a *mastery orientation;* less motivated ones have a *performance orientation.* Those with a mastery orientation are interested in learning new things and in developing their skills. Students who are performance-oriented are concerned with their performance, as it compares with the performances of others. They worry more about their comparative ability than mastering the task. Unfortunately, as Ames (1990) points out, most school experiences tend to reinforce a performance orientation by emphasizing grades, tests, and rank in class.

How can you develop the desirable attitudes? It is not a simple matter. It will take time and patience. You first explain the importance of the attitude. You encourage students to develop that attitude. You model it yourself. You reinforce it with appropriate praise. And you develop a classroom environment that supports the attitudes you are attempting to develop.

Student Skills

Experts who have studied the issue believe that one of the best ways to increase student motivation to learn is to emphasize a metacognitive approach to learning, one that involves students in actively processing information. The main components of this approach are listed below, in the form of advice you would give students. Teaching techniques for developing these skills can be found in several current books that emphasize a cognitive approach to learning. (See, for example, Resnick and Klopfer 1989.)

1. *Prepare to learn.* Focus attention on learning. Set a learning goal that is attainable and challenging. Decide how you will accomplish the learning goal.

2. *Gather and store the information you will need.* Use such strategies as note-taking, underlining, and memory tricks.

3. *Build upon what you already know.* Link the new information with information you already have. Make personal connections with the learning.

4. *Organize what you are learning.* Find patterns and relationships. Show how content is related by using such devices as outlines, web diagrams, and matrices.

5. *Use the knowledge you have acquired to solve important problems.* Develop the habits of mind that make problem-solving meaningful and exciting.

6. *Monitor your learning.* Practice what you are learning. Detect and correct your mistakes.

WHAT CAN YOU DO IN WORKING WITH COLLEAGUES?

You and your colleagues can work together in two ways. First, you can cooperate with the school administrators in changing the school environment so that it is more supportive of student motivation. Here are the main features of such an environment:

- The school emphasizes academic success and high expectations for all students.
- The school involves students in determining policies and rules that affect them directly, within the limits of students' maturity.
- The school recognizes and rewards multiple talents, not just athletic and academic ones.
- The school fosters student attitudes required for high motivation.
- The school empowers teachers, so as to increase their sense of efficacy.

- Teachers are encouraged to take risks and innovate; their performance is not monitored too closely.

Second, you and your colleagues can cooperate in helping each other establish and maintain more motivating

Figure 5-1
KEY FEATURES OF A MOTIVATING CLASSROOM

The teacher in a motivating classroom uses the following instructional practices:

1. Maintains a focus on learning
2. Gives students appropriate choices
3. Conveys reasonably high expectations
4. Uses appropriate routines
5. Stresses informational limits, not controlling ones
6. Provides a motivating physical environment
7. Emphasizes meaningful learning
8. Provides learning tasks that have an optimal degree of ambiguity
9. Is sensitive to, but does not yield to, peer norms
10. Makes effective use of cooperative learning
11. Sets clear and meaningful goals
12. Emphasizes mastery, not performance
13. Stresses intrinsic rewards while making appropriate use of extrinsic ones
14. Works to develop needed student attitudes
15. Teaches the cognitive learning skills

classroom environments. Figure 5-1 summarizes the key features of such an environment.

The best way for you and your colleagues to achieve such an environment is to use your own version of the cooperative development model explained in the previous chapter. There are three cooperative approaches that will be most effective here.

First, you can conduct professional dialogues in which you discuss the features in the chart and share practical strategies for developing motivating classrooms.

Second, you can do some peer coaching. Select one motivating feature to emphasize. Invite a colleague to observe your class, focusing the observation on that particular feature. Then conduct a post-observation conference in which you both discuss the observation and share your perceptions.

Finally, you can use an action-research approach. In this approach, you and your colleagues would identify one group of students whose motivation seems especially low. By reviewing the suggestions in this chapter, you would develop a set of strategies that would seem to be effective. You would implement those strategies and then evaluate their effectiveness.

FOR FURTHER READING

deCharms, R. 1976. *Enhancing motivation: Change in the classroom.* New York: Wiley. A classic work in the field, written by one of the key theorists.

Grossnickle, D.R. and Thihel, W.B. 1988. *Promoting effective student motivation in school and classroom: A practitioner's perspective.* Reston, Vir.: National Association of Secondary School Principals. A practical handbook that makes a complex issue clear and simple.

Purkey, W.W. and Novak, J. 1984. *Inviting school success.* 2d ed. Gives some practical suggestions for making your classroom more inviting and more motivating.

REFERENCES

Ames, C. 1984. Competitive, cooperative, and individualistic goal structures: A cognitive-motivational analysis. In *Research on motivation in education: Student motivation,* vol. 1, eds. R.E. Ames and C. Ames, 171–208. New York: Academic Press.

Ames, C. 1990. Motivation: What teachers need to know. In *Teachers College Record,* vol. 91, 409–21.

Ashton, P. 1985. Motivation and the teacher's sense of efficacy. In *Research on motivation in education: The classroom milieu*, vol.2, eds. R.E. Ames and C. Ames, 141–74. New York: Academic Press.

Brophy, J. 1985. Teachers' expectations, motives, and goals for working with problem students. In *Research on motivation in education: The classroom milieu*, vol.2, eds. R.E. Ames and C. Ames, 175–216. New York: Academic Press.

Covington, M.V. 1984. The motive for self-worth. In *Research on motivation in education: Student motivation*, vol. 1, eds. R.E. Ames and C. Ames, 78–114. New York: Academic Press.

deCharms, R. 1984. Motivation enhancement in educational settings. In *Research on motivation in education: Student motivation*, vol. 1, eds. R.E. Ames and C. Ames, 275–312. New York: Academic Press.

Gagne, E.D. 1985. *The cognitive psychology of school learning*. Boston: Little Brown.

Glatthorn, A.A. 1991. Secondary English classroom environments. In *Handbook of research on teaching the English language arts*; eds. Flood, J.; Jensen, J.M.; Lapp, D.; and Squire, J.R.; 438–56. New York: Macmillan.

Good, T.L. and Brophy, J.E. 1987 *Looking in classrooms*. 4th ed. New York: Harper and Row.

Johnson, D.W.; Johnson, R.T.; Holubec, E.J.; and Roy, P. 1984. *Circles of learning: Cooperation in the classroom*. Alexandria, Vir.: Association for Supervision and Curriculum Development.

Maehr, M.L. 1984. Meaning and motivation: Toward a theory of personal investment. In *Research on motivation in education: Student motivation*, vol. 1, eds. R.E. Ames and C. Ames, 115–44. New York: Academic Press.

Resnick, L.B. and Klopfer, L.E., eds. 1989. *Toward the thinking curriculum: Current cognitive research*. Alexandria, Vir.: Association for Supervision and Curriculum Development.

Ryan, R.M.; Connell, J.P.; and Deci, E.L. 1985. A motivational analysis of self-determination and self-regulation in education. In *Research on motivation in education: The classroom milieu,* vol. 2, eds. R.E. Ames and C. Ames, 13–52. New York: Academic Press.

Slavin, R.E. 1988. Synthesis of research on grouping in elementary and secondary schools. *Educational Leadership* 46(1) 67–77.

Chapter 6

SUPPORTIVE HOME-SCHOOL RELATIONSHIPS

You cannot do the job of fostering learning all by yourself. You and your colleagues need the support of the home—and you and your colleagues, in turn, need to support parents in their efforts to provide a sound home environment for learning. The research is clear that cooperative relationships between home and school make a difference, especially for at-risk students. Telling evidence is provided in a recent study by Caplan, Choy, and Whitmore (1992). Their analysis of why the children of Indochinese refugee families had superior achievement, even when attending distressed urban schools, concluded that family homework-sessions, supervised by the parents, were the most significant factor.

This chapter will explain what you and your colleagues can do in working together to establish a comprehensive parent-involvement program and then focuses on the special contributions that you can make as an individual teacher.

DEVELOP A COMPREHENSIVE PARENT-INVOLVEMENT PROGRAM

Especially in relation to parent involvement, it is almost essential for you and your colleagues to work together with administrators to establish a comprehensive parent-involvement program. While there is much that you can do on your own, the issue is so complex and the benefits so significant that a comprehensive approach is needed. The following guidelines will help you and your colleagues establish an effective program or improve the one you already have in place. They are intended to encourage systematic and reflective planning, rather than to focus on specific activities.

Establish the Organizational Structure

The first step is to develop the necessary organizational structure that will provide the leadership and the planning you need. If your school has an active parent-teacher organization or a parent-advisory council, you can use it as the structure, revitalizing it if necessary. If you have no such group or have only a very inactive one, then you should constitute a special task force, with significant representation of parents, administrators, and classroom teachers to act as an initial organizing structure. In selecting parents for the task force, be sure to work toward a representative diversity of ethnicity and social class. The discussion that follows uses the term *task force* for whatever existing or new group you plan to use in developing a sound program.

Develop Written Policies

As Williams and Chavkin (1989) note, written policies legitimize parent involvement and frame the context for program activities. Therefore, as one of its preliminary steps, the task force should propose its own bylaws and policies; these should be reviewed by the superintendent and approved by the school board because they probably will deal with major policy matters over which the board has legal control.

Develop a Clear Philosophy about Parent Involvement

At the outset, the task force should collaboratively reflect on and articulate a shared philosophy about parent involvement. Here, an analysis by Swap (1990) should be very helpful. She identifies three general philosophies that seem to provide a basis for parent-involvement programs:

1. A philosophy of *school-to-home transmission,* in which educators specify what parents should do at home to support the child's progress at school and to inculcate the values of the dominant culture. With this view, you would essentially tell

parents what they should do to support the school's efforts; you would emphasize one-way communication.

2. A philosophy of *interactive learning*, in which parent-involvement programs focus on two valued outcomes—ensuring student success in the mainstream and valuing the goals and beliefs of the mainstream culture. With this view, you would work with parents to establish continuity between classroom and home and assist parents in understanding the values and the rituals of the school. In addition, you would use parents as resources to help you and your colleagues understand and value the culture of the family.

3. A philosophy of *partnership for school success*, in which parents are welcomed as assets and resources, are respected as equals in the educational enterprise, and are empowered as a means of improving their and their children's lives. As Swap notes, this third philosophy integrates and transcends the first two. There is a shared consensus about goals; the curriculum is revised substantially to reflect multicultural perspectives; and partnerships are established that involve educators, parents, and other community members.

    While this last philosophy seems most desirable from my perspective, it also is the most challenging, requiring major changes in policy and practices. It is therefore vitally important for the task force to reflect upon, discern, articulate its own position.

Identify the Types of Programs Desired

    The next step would be to understand the several types of parent programs that can be developed; such an analysis can assist the task force in deciding where to begin. Obviously, the type of program the task force chooses will reflect its shared philosophy. Here, Epstein and Dauber (1991) have been most helpful in delineating six basic types of parent programs.

91

1. Schools assist families in developing the knowledge and skills needed to provide for children's health and safety, develop parenting skills, and build home conditions that support school learning.

2. Schools communicate with families about school programs and children's progress, through memos, phone calls, report cards, conferences, and other more innovative means.

3. Schools involve parents as resources: parents and other volunteers assist in classrooms and other school areas; family members support student performances, sports, and other events.

4. Schools work with parents in providing learning activities at home by helping parents establish a supportive learning environment, choose appropriate educational programs for their children, and monitor and assist with homework.

5. Parents participate actively in decision-making roles and in serving as advocates for children; the schools assist by training parent leaders.

6. Schools develop and foster collaborative relationships with community organizations and agencies, simplifying family access to social services and developing coordinated programs to use the community as a resource for learning.

Based upon the philosophy already articulated, the task force should determine which one or more of these types it will attempt to plan and implement.

Develop Program Goals

Next, the task force should develop the goals for its programs, deriving those goals from an analysis of its philosophy, its choice of types, and the needs of the school. Those goals will help the task force focus on specific outcomes, rather than simply on undertaking activities. Figure 6-1 shows an example of such a goal statement.

Observe that the goals listed in Figure 6-1 are phrased in a manner that emphasizes collaboration and shared responsibility.

Provide Needed Resources

School administrators should demonstrate their support for the task force by providing initial funding, allocating space and other material resources, and assigning the personnel needed to get the program under way. As Williams and Chavkin (1989) observe, providing these resources is essential for a successful program. Two types of resources seem to be especially crucial, as Epstein (1991) notes: a home-school coordinator, with specific responsibility for coordinating all aspects of the program, and a special room at the school or in the community that parents can call their own. As a general guideline for funding programs, Epstein (1991) recommends a figure of $25 per student to establish a minimal program, with another $10 per pupil for a more extensive one.

Provide Needed Training

School personnel, parents, and community members will need ongoing training, especially if the program is a comprehensive one. Each of the task-force goals could serve as the basis for such training. Here, for example, is the agenda for a series of training sessions related to Goal #2 in Figure 6-1 (Develop a shared understanding of the learning process and how that process can best be facilitated in the home, in the community, and in the school):

1. *What We Know about Learning in the School:* An overview of current research on school factors that affect student achievement.

Figure 6-1
GOAL STATEMENT OF WASHINGTON
SCHOOL/COMMUNITY TASK FORCE

The parents, educators, and other citizens of this community dedicate themselves to working collaboratively to achieve the following outcomes:

1. Develop and implement processes by which all those involved have appropriate input into the decisions made concerning the education of our children and young people.

2. Develop a shared understanding of the learning process and how that process can best be facilitated in the home, in the community, and in the school.

3. Use the community—its places, organizations, and people—as resources for learning.

4. Develop a shared understanding of the nature of human development, especially those aspects that impinge upon pre-school and school learning.

5. Develop a shared understanding of this community—its history, its traditions, its present, and its future.

6. Provide supportive learning environments in the school, in the home, and in the larger community.

7. Develop a shared understanding of the cultures represented in the community and ensure that all cultures are given appropriate attention in the community and in the school.

8. Develop a shared understanding of the culture of the school—its values, ceremonies, rituals, and rules.

9. Communicate openly and productively about educational issues, educational programs, and educational achievement, especially as they impact upon the families of this community and the classrooms in our schools.

10. Foster an extensive program of student activities that will expand and enrich the multiple talents of all students.

2. *What We Know about Learning in the Family:* An overview of how families can work together to foster school learning.

3. *What We Know about Learning in the Community:* An overview of the research on apprenticeships, internships, and volunteer service.

Provide and Evaluate Activities to Achieve Task-Force Goals

Once the task force has identified clear goals, it can begin to plan specific activities. In doing so, members should keep in mind several recommendations based upon sound research. First, plan collaboratively with all participants; do not plan for and then inform parents. Second, do not require that parents always come to the school. In these days when both parents work and when many parents from ethnic minorities feel intimidated by school settings, find ways to take programs to them by using community facilities and arranging for small group meetings in homes. Finally, make use of current technology to communicate with and educate parents. If necessary, provide parents with any resources and/or training they need to use computers, fax machines, and interactive video.

Monitor and Evaluate Systematically

Like all major programs, your home-school program should be systematically evaluated. Someone from the task force should be charged with the responsibility of developing and implementing a program evaluation that includes both formative and summative aspects. The formative aspect should evaluate every activity, monitor the use of funds and other resources, and assess members' participation and satisfaction. Results should be shared with the task force and all other members of the organization as a way to support problem-solving and improvement processes. At certain points in the evaluation cycle, as explained in Chapter 8, a more formal evaluation should be done by using the goals as its basis.

Develop Networks with Other Effective Programs

Home and school organizations can often feel isolated and can easily become convinced that they are struggling on their own to succeed. One way to combat these negative feelings is to form and participate in networks of similar groups. Special resources are listed at the end of this chapter.

Give the Program Time to Mature

Comprehensive programs that involve the restructuring of home and school relationships will need time to develop and mature. Epstein (1991) reports that an excellent program in Indianapolis, Indiana, has been 15 years in the making—and is still growing stronger. While evaluation is necessary, as explained above, premature evaluation that is based on unrealistic expectations for quick results would be counterproductive.

DEVELOP YOUR OWN EFFECTIVE RELATIONSHIPS WITH PARENTS

Even though these school-wide initiatives are essential, they do not take the place of your own actions. As an individual classroom teacher, you can make a major impact on student achievement by using three approaches with parents: by communicating effectively with parents, by using parents in the classroom, and by helping parents provide a supportive learning environment.

Communicate Effectively with Parents

You are probably already an effective communicator with parents; most teachers are. To help you become even more effective, this section will remind you of some basic principles of good teacher-parent communication and then take a closer look at the teacher-parent conference.

Hone Your Communication Skills

Evaluate your own parent-communication practices by checking to see if you follow these basic principles:

1. *The communication is two-way.* In too many instances, schools emphasize a one-way flow: the school sends messages to parents. A two-way flow makes more sense. From time to time meet with groups of parents (on their territory, if necessary) to listen to their concerns. Encourage parents to call you and write to you if they have concerns about their children's progress. In every interaction, listen just as much as you talk.

2. *The communication reflects mutual respect.* You need to show your respect for parents by asking them for their input, by listening openly to their concerns, and by valuing them as useful resources. Avoid such behaviors as the following, which suggest lack of respect: using a condescending or patronizing tone, blaming parents, intruding in family matters without having been asked, using language that implies an ethnic bias (such as, "you people,"or "your ethnic group").

3. The communication is positive as well as problem-identifying. In too many instances, parents hear from the school only when a problem arises. One of many examples of the effective use of positive communication is that provided by Davis (1989). In the school in which he is principal, every teacher identifies two students to honor, one as "students of the week" and one as "super reader of the week." Each identified student receives an award ribbon at the Friday morning assembly; then at night and during the weekend, someone from the school calls the students' parents (speaking in the parents' native language) and tells the parents of the special recognition.

4. *The communication is ongoing.* Rather than relying upon such special occasions as parents' night and parent conferences, effective teachers stay in contact with parents on an ongoing

basis by sending frequent notes, making telephone calls, and sending student work home regularly. Frequent and informal contacts such as these make the parent conference much easier to conduct (Swap 1990).

5. *The communication is clear and audience-sensitive.* As an educator, you feel comfortable in using such jargon as *IEP, CAT,* and *learning disabled.* Keep in mind, however, that educational jargon can sound like a foreign language to many parents. In communicating with parents, put yourself in their shoes and ask yourself: "What would I want to know as a parent?" And in communicating with parents whose native language is other than English, be sure to secure the services of a translator if that seems necessary.

6. *The communication makes effective use of current technology.* Bauch (1989) describes one model that links telephones with computers as a means of encouraging two-way communication. Two technical systems are employed. First, each teacher at the end of the day enters into an electronic mailbox information for parents—learning activities, homework hints, and suggestions for helping children at home. Parents can call in at any time. Second, teachers use a computer-based calling system to store messages in a computer. The messages are then automatically sent to any parent or group of parents the teacher designates. Bauch reports that both teachers and parents are especially pleased with this system.

Conduct Effective Conferences

The parent conference is one of the most popular means of communicating with parents. You can make it more effective by acknowledging the following information, offered by Swap (1990) and Wolf and Stephens (1989).

When it comes to preparing for parent conferences, there are three matters to consider. First, you should view the conference as a two-way exchange of information and a mutual process of solving problems. As you plan for it, keep in mind that you want to make the parent an active participant, not a passive receiver. Second, prepare well for the conference. Swap suggests that early notification (two to three weeks before the conference) is vital. Plan an agenda that allows at least half the time for parents to express their concerns. Assemble any special materials you will need, such as examples of student work.

Next, anticipate difficult moments and rehearse effective ways of dealing with them. Inevitably, you will experience a conference where one or more of the following problems develop: defensiveness, anger, accusation, passive resistance. Practice with a colleague how you would handle such problems and get the colleague's feedback. Also set the stage for an effective conference by providing a conducive physical environment; one that ensures privacy and comfort. (Be sure to provide adult-size chairs; don't expect parents to sit in small pupil desks.)

When conducting the conference, keep in mind the following guidelines: Begin the conference by clarifying your agenda and inviting the parent(s) to contribute to the agenda-setting process. Provide the parent(s) with a brief overview of the child's progress to date and support that general overview with specific examples. Be sure to identify some positive aspects of the child's performance in your class.

If you have observed problems that need attention, identify them as objectively as possible. Here is an example of a good problem-identifying statement:

In my class Jonathan seems to have a problem with his attention span when he reads. When Jonathan reads on his own, he usually reads for a few minutes and then closes the book. I have to remind him several times that he should continue reading. Have you observed at home any similar problems with his ability to read for a longer period of time?

Involve the parent then in developing a collaborative strategy to solve the problem, being sure not to place unrealistic demands on the parents. Remember, parents are not teachers!

Then close the conference by summarizing and looking ahead—what was accomplished and what will be done.

When planning parent conferences, you may wish to involve the student. Hubert (1989) reports that these three-way conferences can be especially effective and can ensure fairness in the conference interactions.

Use Parents in Your Classroom

The second critical way you can work with parents is to involve them directly in your classroom, within the limits of their availability. They can be a very useful adjunct, especially when you have to work with large classes or with special populations.

Plan systematically for such use. First, inform the parents about your general needs. Do you need parents as tutors or student monitors? Then survey the parents to identify any special contributions they can make to the curriculum and the instructional program—solicit information about their special talents, hobbies, careers, and knowledge of ethnic customs and traditions. In the survey, also ask about their availability to assist you with such classroom chores as word processing, copying, and filing. Hunter (1989) recommends that all parent volunteers should meet early in the school year for an orientation and training session. She also provides in her "par-aide" program a carefully structured guide for parents who will be making presentations to the class about their hobbies, careers, or other special knowledge.

Teachers understandably complain about large classes and inadequate resources. Making effective use of parents as volunteers can give you some assistance you critically need and make parents feel valued.

Help Parents Provide a Supportive Learning Environment

The final parent activity you can undertake on your own is to help parents provide a supportive learning environment at home. Through parent conferences and special memos, you can

Figure 6-2
GOOD LEARNING ENVIRONMENTS

Dear Parent/Guardian:

Your home can be a good learning environment for your child. Here are some suggestions that you can use in making your home a place for learning to happen:

1. Limit the amount of television watching that your child does. If children watch too much television, they won't learn as much. As the parent/guardian, you have to decide what is too much. Some experts think that one hour each school day is a good limit.

2. Find a good space that your child can use for studying and doing homework. You don't need a special room. You can set aside any space in your home, such as the kitchen table. Just be sure that your child uses the same space all the time. Be sure it is well lighted. Also be sure it does not have too many things that will take their minds off their studies.

3. Set up a regular schedule for doing homework. Find a time when your child can concentrate and when you can supervise.

4. Be sure that there are good books available for your child to read. Your child can borrow the books from the school library, or you can go with him or her to the community library or book mobile.

5. Find a time when all the family can read together and talk about books. You can all read the same book, or you can read different books. With very young children, someone can read aloud.

6. If your child needs help with school work, let the teacher know. The teacher can locate some special helpers. If there are older school-age children in your family, let them help the younger ones.

7. You should check your child's work just to be sure that all the homework has been done. The school does not expect you to do your child's homework. But taking time to check the homework can help your son or daughter learn that good homework is important.

Figure 6-3
RESEARCH-BASED RECOMMENDATIONS
FOR USING HOMEWORK

1. Be clear about the purposes of assigning homework. Purposes can be to: provide practice, monitor student progress, increase student responsibility, facilitate faster curriculum coverage, increase parent communication, promote high expectations.
2. Assign an appropriate amount of homework. The following guidelines are recommended:

   Grades 1–3: One to three assignments a week, each lasting no more than 15 minutes; in many instances, homework should be voluntary.

   Grades 4–6: Two to four assignments a week, each lasting 15–45 minutes, emphasizing reading and mathematics; total daily time should not exceed one hour.

   Grades 7–8: Homework regularly assigned, not necessarily daily, emphasizing reading and mathematics; total daily assignments should not require more than two hours, including study time at school.

   Grades 9–12: Daily homework for most high school courses, with an emphasis on completing moderate assignments well. Weekend and holiday homework should be limited to review, make-up, or voluntary assignments.

3. Do not give homework as a punishment and do not use "no homework" as a reward.
4. Be sure that students have the understanding and skills needed to do the homework successfully. Do not use homework to present new material or complex skills.
5. Do not expect parents to assist with homework; make clear that their responsibility is to provide a good study environment and to check to see that homework is being done.
6. Establish and enforce an accountability system for homework. Do not accept incomplete homework. Provide additional remedial homework for those who do not complete assignments.
7. Use homework results diagnostically, to identify the type and extent of mislearning. Give feedback on homework, but do not use homework as a test of knowledge.

SOURCES: Butler 1987, Cooper 1989.

educate them about the type of environment children need. Figure 6-2 is an example of material you can share with parents; it is worded so that you can copy and distribute it at parent meetings.

A key part of a supportive learning environment in the home is regular homework time. Here, you can play a very vital role by making homework effective. Figure 6-3 lists some research-based suggestions for making homework a productive part of the total learning experience.

CONCLUDING NOTE

Like all teachers, you have a difficult and demanding job. Effective home and school programs can provide you and your colleagues with excellent resources.

FOR FURTHER READING

Rather than suggest books to read in this area, I think it would be more useful to provide you and your colleagues with the names and addresses of several organizations active in the field. They can provide you with several types of materials.

Center on Parent Involvement. Johns Hopkins University, 3505 N. Charles Street, Baltimore, Md. 21218.

Home and School Institute. 1201 16th Street, N.W., Washington, D.C. 20036.

Institute for Responsive Education. 605 Commonwealth Avenue, Boston, Mass. 02215.

National Coalition for Parent Involvement in Education. 119 N. Payne Street, Alexandria, Vir. 22314.

National Committee for Citizens in Education. 10840 Little Patuxent Parkway, #301, Columbia, Md. 21044.

National School Volunteer Association. 701 N. Fairfax Street, #320, Alexandria, Vir. 22314.

REFERENCES

Bauch, J.P. 1989. The TransParent School Model: New technology for parent involvement. *Educational Leadership*, 47(2): 32–4.

Butler, J.A. 1987. *Homework*. Portland, Ore.: Northwest Regional Educational Laboratory.

Caplan, N., Choy, M.H., and Whitmore, J.K. 1992. Indochinese refugee families and academic achievement. *Scientific American*, 266(2): 36–44.

Cooper, H.M. 1989. *Homework*. White Plains, N.Y.: Longman.

Davis, B.C. 1989. A successful parent involvement program. *Educational Leadership*, 47(2): 21–3.

Epstein, J.L. 1991. Paths to partnership. *Phi Delta Kappan*, vol. 72, 344–49.

Epstein, J.L. and Dauber, S.L. 1991. School programs and teacher practices of parent involvement in inner-city elementary and middle schools. *Elementary School Journal*, vol. 91, 289–305.

Hubert, B.D. 1989. Students belong in the "parent-teacher" conference, too. *Educational Leadership*, 47(2): 29.

Hunter, M. 1989. Join the "par-aide" in education. *Educational Leadership*, 47(2): 36–9.

Swap, S.M. 1990. *Parent involvement and success for all children: What we know now.* Boston: Institute for Responsive Education.

Williams, D.L., Jr. and Chavkin, N.F. 1989. Essential elements of strong parent involvement programs. *Educational Leadership*, 47(2): 18–20.

Wolf, J.S. and Stephens, T.M. 1989. Parent/teacher conferences: Finding common ground. *Educational Leadership*, 47(2): 28–31.

Chapter 7

A LEARNING-CENTERED SCHEDULE

Although many professors of school administration seem to sneer at schedule making as only a minor "technical" skill, it is instead a crucial aspect of school effectiveness. Essentially, the schedule is the mechanism by which resources are allocated—time, space, and personnel. In a sense, they who control the schedule, control the school's resources. This chapter argues for a learning-centered schedule and shows how you and your colleagues can make your school's schedule more facilitative of student learning.

THE NATURE OF A LEARNING-CENTERED SCHEDULE

To understand the goal of your efforts in this area, you need to know what constitutes a good schedule. The key attributes are listed in Figure 7-1 and discussed below, first in general terms and then more specifically.

The first general observation to note about these attributes is that many of them contradict each other. For example, if the only consideration is to maximize learning time, then teachers would have no planning time. If a teachable assignment that reflects teacher preferences is all that matters, then many teachers would have homogeneous classes. These contradictions suggest that the schedule-making process is essentially a negotiation of trade-offs, with the goal being to arrive at the best combination of several compromises.

The second point to recognize is that these attributes are operationalized in a somewhat differential manner, depending upon school level and type of schedule. Elementary teachers in a self-contained classroom and middle school teachers with a block-of-time schedule can make many of these decisions on their own. High school teachers who cope with a complex period schedule face more troublesome constraints.

Let's turn our attention now to the specific issues identified in Figure 7-1.

The first and most important consideration is that the schedule maximizes instructional time and reflects curricular priorities. Noninstructional time (such as homeroom periods) should be kept to a bare minimum. Elementary and middle school teachers should allocate time to the several subjects they teach on the basis of the school's curricular priorities, not on their own preferences. This guideline is especially significant for elementary mathematics and science. The research in general suggests that many elementary teachers give relatively little time to those subjects because they feel poorly prepared to teach them.

Time allocations are important also within a subject, once the schedule has been set. Consider, for example, two fifth grade teachers planning their language-arts period. One gives a great deal of time to the study of formal grammar and slights the teaching of writing; the other gives no time to the teaching of formal grammar and increases the time given to the teaching of writing. Their students' achievements reflect the way the teachers have allocated time: the first class learns formal grammar, a minimally useful body of knowledge without writing skills; the second class learns to write, an essential means of communication, but one that would be more effective with adequate knowledge of grammar.

Once time allocations for instruction have been made, then administrators and teachers should cooperate in defending instructional time. They should make an explicit contract with each other to keep to an absolute minimum intrusive behaviors, such as calling students from a class, shortening classes because of special assemblies, dismissing students early for extracurricular activities, and interrupting classes with messages and announcements. While teachers often blame administrators for such

Figure 7-1

CHARACTERISTICS OF A LEARNING-CENTERED SCHEDULE

1. *The schedule maximizes instructional time.* The schedule reflects curricular priorities and gives first priority to students' learning needs. Administrators and teachers cooperate in defending instructional time.

2. *The schedule facilitates the professional growth of teachers.* Teachers have time to plan collaboratively and to cooperate in fostering their professional growth.

3. *The schedule reflects grouping practices that do not stigmatize students.* It gives all students access to a quality curriculum and fosters student achievement.

4. *The schedule gives teachers a teachable situation.* Teachers are assigned to their area of specialization. Wherever possible, teacher preferences about the number and type of preparations and room assignments are acknowledged. Classes are neither too large nor excessively heterogeneous.

5. *The schedule is flexible and learning-oriented.* Time is organized according to learning needs, instead of learning being constrained by rigid time frameworks.

6. *The schedule is responsive to the needs of students and teachers.* Sufficient time is provided for relaxing, eating, and taking care of personal needs.

SOURCES: Anderson 1984, Dempsey and Traverso 1983, Glatthorn 1986.

practices, many teachers seem to operate on this principle: "No class intrusions—except when I want them."

The second characteristic is almost as important as the first. If teachers are to become truly professional as collaborative leaders, they will need increased time for planning and professional growth. As Little (1990) points out, in many schools the schedule is made without reference to teachers' professional growth needs and the school's need for collaborative planning for school improvement. A recent study of teachers' working conditions concluded that 64 percent of the responding teachers reported they had less than one hour each day of preparation time or no time at all (Carnegie Foundation for the Advancement of Teaching 1990). In the most effective schools, special time is provided so that teachers can plan collaboratively, implement peer-coaching programs, undertake action research, and work together with the principal on school-improvement programs (Glatthorn 1986).

Currently, schools provide such special time in several ways. Teacher aides and volunteers take over classes. Classes are combined for special assembly programs. The principal and the assistant principal substitute for teachers. And, from time to time, half-day substitutes are used to provide longer periods of time for staff development and collaborative planning. Obviously, all these are compromises that take teachers away from their students, but the payoff seems to be worth the sacrifices.

The way students are grouped for learning is also a critical matter. Because grouping has been so often oversimplified and distorted, it would make sense to clarify three related terms before recommending solutions.

Tracking is assigning students to a stratified sequence of courses, with a particular post-high school focus, such as *general* or *vocational* or *college preparatory. Between-class grouping* is assigning students to a particular class on the basis of the student's achievement in that subject. Thus, a school might have three levels of mathematics, ranked by ability in mathematics. *Within-class grouping* is a process by which a teacher groups students within a class for certain instructional purposes. For example, most elementary teachers divide their classes into three reading groups.

Although many educators are inclined to make the sweeping generalization that "ability grouping is completely wrong," a closer look at the research and the realities of teaching suggest the issue is more complex than it seems. Figure 7-2 presents a summary of that research.

School systems that are trying to find the best accommodation to a very complicated education problem have arrived at several compromises. First, they minimize tracking at the high school, providing only two tracks: academic and tech-prep. The tech-prep program emphasizes a high quality program in the core subjects along with technical education for students who aspire to such careers. Second, they provide an accelerated curriculum for the most gifted, who are grouped for special instruction. They use heterogeneous grouping as a basis for assigning students to classes but attempt to reduce the range of abilities in any given class.

This set of decisions should not be seen as the best answer to this complex problem. It suggests instead that you and your colleagues need to study the problem very carefully and work out a solution that results in better achievement without stigmatizing students who are deficient in verbal or mathematical abilities.

You and your colleagues also need a teachable situation. You know what a teachable situation is: class size is manageable; the ability range is not too extreme; you are teaching in the area for which you have prepared; you have access to good facilities, materials, and equipment; students are not disruptive. The data suggest that the profession is far from achieving that desired state. Here are some selected findings from a recent study by the Carnegie Foundation for the Advancement of Teaching:

- Teachers who report they are assigned to teach subjects for which they are unqualified: 18 percent
- Teachers who say general support services for teaching

111

Figure 7-2
SUMMARY OF THE RESEARCH ON ABILITY GROUPING

1. Curriculum tracking has several serious weaknesses. It results in the stratification of the student body on the basis of social class. It often delivers an impoverished curriculum to low-ability tracks. And in most tracking systems, there is little student mobility (Oakes 1985).

2. Ability grouping for the gifted seems effective, especially if it results in an accelerated curriculum (Rogers 1991).

3. In a classroom where competition is emphasized, the presence of students perceived as having low ability is a source of motivation for high ability students; however, the presence of high ability students decreases motivation for low ability students (Nicholls 1979).

4. Classes of extreme heterogeneity pose special problems for teachers; such classes are often more difficult for the teacher to manage and to individualize instruction (Evertson and Hickman 1981).

5. In general, heterogeneous between-class grouping seems to achieve better cognitive and affective results for most students (Slavin 1987).

6. Within-class grouping seems most effective in teaching mathematics. However, in teaching beginning reading, some form of the Joplin plan (where students are reassigned on the basis of reading ability) seems most effective (Slavin 1987).

are only fair or poor: 59 percent

- Teachers who spend their own money for supplies and materials: 96 percent (average expenses: $250 per term)
- Teachers who report their classes are too large: 38 percent
- Teachers who believe their office space is fair, poor, or not available: 75 percent
- Teachers who report that disruptive student behavior is a somewhat serious or serious problem in their school: 86 percent

Obviously, many of these conditions result from starved school district budgets—a situation that is not easily changed. However, a nation that found the money to fight the Gulf War can surely find the money to educate its children—if it really believes in their future.

The fifth guideline involves the flexible use of time. The best schedules serve the requirements of the teaching/learning transaction. Unfortunately, in most schools, learning is controlled by the schedule. In this sense, the elementary teacher in the self-contained classroom has the most desirable schedule. Teams of middle school teachers who are assigned a block of time that they can use flexibly also have this advantage. It is high school teachers who suffer the most here. If you wanted to devise the worst possible schedule for learning, you probably would propose the standard high school schedule: 45 minutes a day for all subjects, with an occasional double period.

Dissatisfaction with the *status quo* has led many high schools to experiment with such flexible arrangements as the following: modular schedules (in which the schedule is built upon short time increments, such as 15-minute modules); block-of-time schedules (in which a team of teachers is assigned a long block of time to divide as it sees fit); rotating period schedules (in which a class that meets first period on Monday would meet on second period Tuesday, and so on); and the six-day cycle (in which the schedule is rotated every sixth day, instead of on a weekly basis).

While such schedules may seem only to tinker with the standard schedule, a more radical approach has surfaced in the *Copernican Plan*, devised by Carroll (1990). The Copernican Plan provides for long blocks of time for intensive study. In one version of the plan, a student would study only two subjects at a time—one in the morning and one in the afternoon—for a 12-week period. Although the plan was initiated with great fanfare, recent news reports indicate that full implementation has been deferred for lack of funds.

The final guideline is a common-sense reminder that students and teachers are ordinary human beings who need time to relax, to eat, and to take care of personal needs. In the desire to increase instructional time, some schools have unwisely ignored these needs by reducing the length of the lunch period, cutting back on recess time, and requiring teachers to give up their planning period in order to "cover" for a teacher who has to leave early.

DEVELOPING A LEARNING-CENTERED SCHEDULE

How can you and your colleagues work toward a schedule that is more learning-centered? Let's look first at what all of you can do together in working with the principal—and then at what you can do on your own.

Collective Action for Learning-Centered Schedules

You will first need an organizational structure for accomplishing your goals—either an existing committee or a special task force. The first job of the committee or task force would be to identify the limits within which it has to work; such limits are typically set by the state and the local school board in specifying the minimum number of instructional hours for all schooling, the subjects to be offered, and—in many cases—the minimum number of hours for each subjects.

Task-force members should then review the research cited here as well as other sources they identify to build their knowledge base. They should summarize their knowledge base in a two- or three-page handout that can be distributed to the entire faculty for its input.

With those jobs accomplished, the task force should examine the following issues, usually in the order listed:

1. *How shall we organize the program of studies for each grade?* The "program of studies," as the term is used here, is the total set of educational offerings for a given group of students. Answering this question demands that the task force resolve such specific issues as: what subjects will be required, which elective offerings will be made available, how much curriculum integration will be provided, and how much time will be allocated to each subject.

2. *How shall we assign students to this program of studies?* The central question here, of course, is whether students should be grouped on a homogeneous or heterogeneous basis. The issue also involves a determination as to whether a "mini-school," "alternative program," "school-within-a-school" or other similar approach should be used to divide large schools into smaller units. Here, it often makes sense to give teams of teachers across the school the responsibility of providing instruction for approximately the same number of students. This responsibility includes making decisions about specific class sizes and teacher loads within the assigned group of students and teachers. In some large schools, it has been possible to give one teacher per group the responsiblities of a department director along with a sharply reduced teaching schedule simply by increasing other class sizes by five or six.

3. *How shall we staff for this program of studies?* This question involves such matters as whether teachers work together as

teams, how teachers are assigned to subjects and groups of students, and how specialists (such as art, music, and physical education teachers) are used. In examining this issue, the committee should keep in mind the special needs of novice teachers. More than anyone else, they need a teachable situation to cope with the demands of the first year of teaching. In too many schools, teacher seniority dictates how teacher preferences are respected; thus, the beginners get the most difficult classes, and the older hands get the easier assignments.

4. *What type of schedule will give the instructional staff the flexibility it needs in maximizing learning?* It is at this stage that the task force should examine the scheduling alternatives described earlier, keeping in mind that the most complicated schedule is not necessarily the best one.

5. *How should space be allocated for maximum learning?* Space is always in short supply. And in too many instances, decisions about it are made on the basis of power and seniority. There is a need instead for professional deliberation about such issues as the following: What are the special space needs of specific subjects and how can they best be accommodated? How can we allocate space so that "floating" is minimized? What space can we make available for teacher planning and other professional activities? How can space allocation foster collegial interaction?

6. *How can we best accommodate the personal needs of students as well as the personal and professional needs of teachers?* Here, the committee needs to be creative, especially in finding ways for teachers to have extended planning periods. One practical goal would be to provide every teacher with a single planning period on each of four days and two back-to-back planning periods on one day of the week. That double period would be set aside for team planning, with specific guidelines about its use.

Based upon its study of these issues, the task force would then make recommendations to the entire faculty for further discussion and modifications.

WHAT YOU CAN DO WORKING ON YOUR OWN

Even if these major changes do not seem feasible in your school, there are still several steps you can take personally to develop your own "learning-centered schedule."

The first step is to develop your own time allocations. If you are an elementary teacher, then you have two responsibilities here. The first is to allocate time to the separate subjects you are expected to teach. If your school system or school does not provide guidelines, then you might consider these recommendations made by Goodlad (1984): reading and language arts, one and one-half hours each day; mathematics, one hour each day; social studies, two and one-half hours each week; science, two and one-half hours each week; health and physical education, two and one-half hours each week; arts, three and one-half hours each week. If you decide to integrate reading, language arts, and social studies, then make the block of time reflect the sum of the individual allotments.

The second responsibility is one shared by all teachers, elementary and secondary. That is to allocate time within a particular subject so that it reflects curricular priorities. The best way to accomplish this task is to develop a yearly schedule. Begin by reflecting on and reviewing several sources of information: the curriculum guide, the textbook, any required tests, your knowledge of the subject, the recommendations of experts, and your knowledge of the students.

Then use all that information to divide the curriculum for that year into a sequence of instructional units. Some of those units might be integrated around a general theme, such as "Families First"; some might focus on a given aspect of the subject, such as "Map Reading." Allocate time to these units in a manner that reflects the priorities you have established for your students in that subject. In developing a yearly planning calendar of this sort, keep in mind that depth is better than superficial coverage. If you want to teach problem-solving and critical thinking, you need extended periods of time. That means you may have to omit some less important content.

With those time allocations established for separate subjects and for components of a single subject, turn to your use of time in the classroom. At this point, you probably expect to hear a sermon about increasing "time on task." There is no need for such a sermon, for two reasons. First, you have heard about time on task so much that it does not need repeating.

The second reason is more important. You should be chiefly concerned with the *quality* of learning, not the *quantity*. Instead of being unduly concerned about "How much time on task?" you and your colleagues should be asking instead, "What is the quality of the task?"

To understand this matter, consider two classes:

In Class A, the teacher seems almost obsessed with increasing time on task. He starts class promptly, takes care of business quickly, keeps youngsters busily engaged by close monitoring, makes smooth transitions, and ends just when the bell rings. However, all during that high-task lesson, the students are working on drill-and-practice materials that emphasize low-level comprehension of textbook knowledge.

Now in Class B, the teacher is more relaxed. He begins class with a few minutes of talk about last night's basketball game. He seems a bit slow in passing out materials. The transitions are a little rough. And he ends a few minutes early. But throughout the lesson, he has had the students engaged in high quality learning: they are using knowledge to solve problems, working together cooperatively, and actively communicating with each other.

Class B is the type of class you should want, with perhaps

a little tightening. You want quality learning—not boring, mindless practice. Here are some signs that indicate quality learning is taking place:

- The students are working hard. You are facilitating their learning by acting as a cognitive coach—providing the structure they need, modeling, giving cues. But, students are doing most of the work. (Have you ever noticed that in the usual class the teacher does all the work?)

- The students are solving problems, using what the psychologists call *generative knowledge*—knowledge that is used, applied, worked with. You are minimizing *inert knowledge*—knowledge that lies fallow because it is not used.

- The students are asking questions. (In your next lesson, ask one of your students just to count the number of times a student in your class asks a question.) You are stimulating their curiosity, prodding them to ask questions, and rewarding those who ask questions.

- The students are using language as a means of learning: they are talking in small groups and using writing as a means of learning. You are encouraging and monitoring such use.

- The students are engaged in assessing their learning. They are evaluating their own work and the work of their classmates. You are monitoring these student assessments and adding your own, using the assessment process as a means of facilitating learning.

- Finally, and most important of all, the students are learning something significant. When they leave your classroom, they are smarter than when they entered—about something that matters.

FOR FURTHER READING

Anderson, L.W., ed. 1984. *Time and school learning.* New York: St. Martin's Press. Perhaps the best single source on the use and importance of school time.

Oakes, J. 1985. *Keeping track: How schools structure inequality.* New Haven, Conn.: Yale University Press. The classic work on the insidious effects of curriculum tracking.

Sizer, T.R. 1992. *Horace's school: Redesigning the American high school.* Boston: Houghton Mifflin. A challenging book about what schools could be if we became serious about educational reform.

REFERENCES

Carnegie Foundation for the Advancement of Teaching. 1990. *The condition of teaching: A state-by-state analysis.* Princeton, N.J.: Carnegie Foundation for the Advancement of Teaching.

Carroll, J.M. 1990. The Copernican Plan: Restructuring the American high school. *Phi Delta Kappan,* vol. 71, 358–65.

Dempsey, R.A. and Traverso, H.P. 1983. *Scheduling the secondary school.* Reston, Vir.: National Association of Secondary School Principals.

Evertson, C.M. and Hickman, R.C. 1981. *The tasks of teaching classes of varied group composition.* Austin, Tex.: Research and Development Center for Teacher Education, University of Texas.

Glatthorn, A.A. 1986. How does the school schedule affect the curriculum? In *Rethinking reform: The principal's dilemma,* eds. H.J. Walberg and J.W. Keef, 53-60. Reston, Vir.: National Association of Secondary School Principals.

Goodlad, J.I. 1984. *A place called school: Prospects for the future.* New York: McGraw-Hill.

Little, J.W. 1990. Conditions of professional development in secondary schools. In *The contexts of teaching in secondary schools,* eds. M.W. McLaughlin, J.E. Talbert, and N. Bascia; 187–223. New York: Teachers College Press.

Nicholls, J. 1979. Quality and equality in intellectual development: The role of motivation in education. *American Psychologist,* vol. 34, 1071–84.

Oakes, J. 1985. *Keeping track: How schools structure inequality.* New Haven, Conn.: Yale University Press.

Rogers, K.B. 1991. *The relationship of grouping practices to the education of the gifted and talented learner.* Storrs, Conn.: National Research Center on the Gifted and Talented, University of Connecticut.

Slavin, R.E. 1987. Ability grouping and student achievement in the elementary schools: A best evidence synthesis. *Review of Educational Research*, vol. 57, 292–336.

Chapter 8

A VALID AND COMPREHENSIVE ASSESSMENT SYSTEM

You probably hear a great deal of talk these days about assessing students and evaluating teachers. You don't hear too much talk about assessing school climate and evaluating principals. This chapter argues for a comprehensive approach to assessment that uses valid measures and systematically assesses all components of the school. It first describes what a comprehensive evaluation program might entail and then takes a closer look at the two special aspects that most involve you: evaluation of student learning and evaluation of teachers.

DEVELOP A COMPREHENSIVE EVALUATION PROGRAM

You and your colleagues should work together with the school administrators to develop a comprehensive evaluation program that meets the following criteria:

- The evaluation program systematically examines all major components of school improvement.
- The evaluation program is coordinated with the school district's evaluation program and with evaluations by accrediting agencies.
- The evaluation program is technically sound. It uses multiple measures and multiple data sources, focuses on the key issues, and makes use of valid and reliable instruments.
- The evaluation program does not over-tax district or school resources.
- The evaluation program produces data that are used for ongoing school improvement.

Figure 8-1 shows one possible design (schedule) for an eight-year program. Obviously, it is only an example; each school would analyze its own local conditions. Several points need to be clarified about what the schedule represents. First, all the substantive program components discussed in this book would be evaluated on a rotating cycle, spread across the eight-year period so as not to overload the system. In each case, it is a rigorous and systematic evaluation, supplemented where necessary with less rigorous formative ones. For example, the professional development programs would receive a rigorous evaluation every third or fourth year.

Three groups of personnel are also evaluated: (1) the leadership team, (2) probationary teachers and marginally competent tenured teachers, and (3) competent tenured teachers.

The leadership team is evaluated every fourth year. This evaluation would assess the performance of individuals, such as the principal, the assistant principal, and department chairs. It would also assess the overall performance of the team as a group. Probationary teachers and marginally competent tenured teachers are evaluated each year. Competent tenured teachers are divided into four cohorts; each cohort is evaluated once every four years. Student achievement is evaluated each year.

Finally, once every six years, prior to the visit from the accreditation team, a comprehensive evaluation of the entire program is undertaken. During that sixth year, no other program component is evaluated—only personnel. Note that the comprehensive evaluation should be a relatively simple matter because components have been evaluated on an ongoing basis.

Obviously, designing, planning, and implementing such an evaluation design is a complex technical undertaking that requires significant expertise. The important matter to stress here is your responsibility in identifying the need for such a comprehensive design, not in carrying it out.

Figure 8-1
SCHEDULE FOR A COMPREHENSIVE EVALUATION PROGRAM

	Year 1	Year 2	Year 3	Year 4	Year 5	Year 6	Year 7	Year 8
Curriculum			X				X	
Professional Development Programs				X				X
Motivation Programs			X	X				X
Home/School Relations			X			X		
Schedule					X			
Foundation Elements				X				X
Leadership	X				X			
Probationary Teachers	X	X	X	X	X	X	X	X
Tenured Teachers*	A	B	C	D	A	B	C	D
Student Learning	X	X	X	X	X	X	X	X
Comprehensive Evaluation						X		

* Competent tenured teachers are divided into four cohorts (A–D). Each cohort is evaluated once every four years.

125

USE A SYSTEMATIC PROCESS TO EVALUATE STUDENT LEARNING

Teachers spend a great deal of time and effort evaluating student learning. Too often that time and effort are misdirected, resulting in an evaluation process that does not play a productive role in learning. To assist you in making more effective use of evaluation, this section will emphasize the use of evaluation as a key aspect of the learning process.

Using Diagnostic Evaluations

Diagnostic evaluation, as previously noted, obtains evaluation information in order to make some tentative decisions about placement and planning in advance of the instructional process. In this sense, diagnostic evaluation assesses present learning in order to make future learning more productive. Diagnostic evaluation can be used at the beginning of a unit to ascertain students' present level of knowledge and to make appropriate modifications in curriculum content and instructional methodology. However, its more important use is at the beginning of the school year, when it can yield some essential information with regard to several crucial issues. The major issues are identified as follows and will organize our discussion of diagnostic evaluation.

Grouping Decisions

Diagnostic evaluation can be used to answer this question: If within-class grouping is to be used, to which group should the student initially be assigned in this subject for the coming year? Decisions about within-class grouping, typically used in elementary reading and mathematics, should be made tentatively on the basis of the diagnostic results. Those initial placement decisions should be reviewed periodically throughout the year, as you get additional performance data.

The decision about grouping can be made with some validity by relying upon the recommendations of the teacher from the previous year and by checking standardized and end-of-year test results. You can also use a teacher-made test to determine grouping. If you use a test to determine grouping, Berliner (1987) recommends that you include a wide-ranging set of questions of different degrees of difficulty. The results from such a test will yield comprehensive information about students' cognitive functioning.

You should also be sure to use appropriate performance measures in the diagnostic process. A performance measure is a means of assessing learning by requiring the student to demonstrate or perform some desired behavior. Here are some performance measures you can use in the diagnostic process: ask the students to write about a specific issue; ask the students to explain orally how they solved a problem; ask the students to indicate how they would respond in a simulated context; ask the students to demonstrate their ability to perform some psychomotor skill.

Students should be grouped on the basis of ability in a specific aspect of the curriculum, not on the basis of group size or total numbers. Unfortunately, many teachers are more concerned with achieving similar group size. Hallinan and Sorenson (1983) note that most teachers form three groups and try to keep their sizes equal, rather than grouping on the basis of ability alone.

Basic Skills Readiness

The next diagnostic issue is whether the student has the reading and writing skills needed to learn the subject involved during the coming year. As Bloom, Hastings, and Madaus (1971) note, such skills are essential in learning most academic subjects; and early remediation is critical.

Here the student's cumulative folder and assessment portfolio can be helpful. A careful analysis of the student's scores on standardized reading tests and the student's end-of-year writing assignments can help you determine if special remediation is needed in these areas. You can also use a very simple diagnostic performance measure of reading ability: ask the student to read a section of the chapter in the text and then summarize what was read.

Entry Skills and Knowledge

The third diagnostic issue is whether the student has mastered the subject-specific skill and knowledge that the coming year's work requires. Keep in mind here that the focus is on the coming year's work. If you are a seventh grade teacher, you need not be concerned with determining whether the students have mastered all the skills and knowledge taught in the sixth grade curriculum; that was the job of the sixth grade teacher. Instead, you should be concerned with whether the students have the skills and knowledge needed to achieve well in the seventh grade program.

The importance of this issue varies with the subject. The mathematics curriculum in general is highly sequential: the eighth grade mathematics curriculum typically requires the student to have mastered many of the concepts and skills taught in the seventh grade. This is not the case, however, in social studies. The social studies curriculum typically is constructed without much concern for sequential grade-to-grade development. If the student can read and write well and knows some basic social studies skills (such as map reading), he or she can do reasonably well handling the new curriculum.

There are two useful ways to develop an entry-level assessment. One way is to analyze very carefully the curriculum you are expected to teach in the coming year. Focus especially on the initial units. Ask yourself this question: "What skills and knowledge do my students need to have in order to deal with these initial units?"

The second way is to rely on the curriculum guide for the previous year. Review that guide and identify the skills and knowledge objectives emphasized; then determine which objectives seem important in the year to come.

Either method should give you the information you need to develop an entry- level diagnostic test. Bloom, Hastings, and Madaus (1971) recommend that diagnostic tests include a large number of relatively easy items—items that 65 percent or more of the class would get correct. They also suggest that at higher grade levels where end-of-year tests are given, the teacher can administer at the start of the year an alternative form of the end-of-year test, to determine how much students already know about that year's work.

You can then review individual and class results to answer these questions:

1. Which skills and knowledge will need to be reviewed for the entire class?
2. Which individual students need special remediation for skills and knowledge that the rest of the class has mastered?

Learning Styles

Several experts in the field also recommend that the teacher diagnose each student's learning-style preferences and use the results to modify instructional approaches. Several learning-style assessment instruments are available; Guild and Garger's (1985) publication examines six of the most widely used instruments. And Dunn and Griggs' (1988) work reports on nine secondary schools that have successfully implemented special programs designed to respond to learning-style differences.

There is at present some controversy over the value of assessing learning styles. On the one hand, there exists a considerable body of evidence suggesting that accommodating students' learning-style preferences improves their achievement and attitudes. Dunn, Beaudry, and Klavas (1989) summarize their synthesis of the research with this strong conclusion:

> When permitted to learn difficult academic information or skills through their identified preferences, children tend to achieve statistically higher test and attitude scores than when instruction is dissonant with their preferences (p. 56).

129

On the other hand, there are several critics of the learning-styles movement who express cautions about accommodating learning-style differences. In what seems to be an objective review of the issue, Curry (1990) identifies four pervasive problems with the research on learning styles. The first is the bewildering array of definitions and conceptualizations of learning styles; such definitions vary so much and are often so vague that it is difficult to know whether they are in fact measuring the same thing.

The second problem is what Curry terms the "weakness in the accumulated evidence for the reliability and validity of measurements" (p. 51). She notes that few of the instruments used in the research on learning styles have been carefully evaluated for validity and reliability. Related to this issue is the weakness of the empirical evidence on the effectiveness of accommodating to style preferences. She notes that most of the supportive studies were doctoral dissertations conducted under faculty with a vested interest in substantiating their own approach; the studies have also been poorly designed; and data have not been analyzed with sufficient care.

Finally, Curry concludes that researchers have just not resolved the over-riding question of whether optimal results are achieved when learning styles are systematically matched or systematically mismatched.

The absence of conclusive findings about this issue suggests that you should not make major instructional or grouping decisions based upon the results of one style inventory. The issue would, however, be an excellent one for you and your colleagues to study together in an action-research mode.

USING EVALUATION FOR ACCOUNTABILITY PURPOSES

A vital part of establishing a supportive learning environment is developing and implementing an accountability system. Students need to believe that they are being held

130

accountable for their learning, especially when this learning involves seatwork, group work, and homework.

Evaluation can play a useful role here. When planning work of this sort, you should determine in advance how you will evaluate the results. Here are some of the choices available to you:

- An oral report by the students
- An oral quiz
- A written quiz
- An assessment of a product produced as an outcome of independent work
- An assessment through observations of students at work
- The evaluation of student performance or demonstration

It is especially important to evaluate homework. The evaluation can emphasize the accountability purpose and can also give you useful information about problems students encountered. Butler's (1987) review of the research leads her to recommend very strongly that all homework be corrected routinely and quickly and that incomplete homework not be accepted.

However, because checking all homework can be tedious for both students and the teacher, you should vary the methods you use to evaluate the completion and success of homework. Here are some useful suggestions (Butler 1987, Glatthorn 1991).

1. Send selected students to put a portion of their homework on the chalkboard while you orally quiz the rest. Then involve the entire class in checking the homework on the board.

2. Conduct a brief rapid-fire oral quiz on the homework.

3. Collect all the homework at the start of the class (to be checked later for completion), quiz students on homework content, and ask them to identify homework problems.

4. Have all students do new work related to homework concepts and correct such work in class.

Using Evaluation for Instructional Purposes

One of the most important uses of evaluation is to guide the instructional process. In this sense, evaluation is not perceived as something separate from instruction; instead, it is viewed as an integral part of teaching. In almost every lesson, the effective teacher uses an interactive and recursive process: assess-plan-teach-assess-modify plans-teach.

The research on effective monitoring of student learning suggests that the following practices can be used in almost every lesson. (The discussion that follows draws primarily from Bloom, Hastings, and Madaus 1971; Good and Brophy 1987; Guskey 1985; and Berliner 1987.)

First, begin the instructional session with a brief oral or written quiz that checks students' knowledge of skills and knowledge taught in prior lessons. If you use a written quiz, have students check their own work or each other's, emphasizing that the quiz has only an instructional purpose for you and them. If you use oral quizzing, keep your questions and responses brief.

Second, as you explain a concept or skill, monitor attentiveness by observing student behavior, remembering that such monitoring does not always yield reliable results. Do not be misled by students who have mastered the art of concealing inattentiveness by giving signals of being on task.

Next, after you have explained a concept or demonstrated a skill, check for students' understanding. The easiest way is to ask a few specific questions, being sure not to call upon only those who volunteer. You can ask younger students to use certain previously established signals, such as "thumbs up/thumbs down," or " hold up one finger if the first answer is correct, two if the second." Or with reluctant or less able students, you can ask for a group response.

132

If you have students work in groups, monitor this work closely. Hold students accountable for the productive use of time.

Also, from time to time, evaluate individual learning by asking each student to write a brief response to a question or to write a description of a concept. Such written responses help students clarify their own understandings and give you useful feedback.

Finally, close class with a brief evaluation of what has been learned. You can use several methods for this end-of-class evaluation—conduct a brief oral quiz, use a written quiz, or require all students to write a summary of the lesson's highlights.

In addition to using these guidelines for each class, keep in mind some general practices. First, remember that the primary purpose of such evaluation is to improve learning. Use errors as opportunities for learning. Second, follow up the instructional evaluation with appropriate feedback to the students and additional help when that is indicated. Third, use the evaluation to modify your own instructional approaches. If it is obvious that most of the students have not understood a concept you just explained, the fault probably lies with your teaching, not with their learning. Finally, build in as often as you can opportunities for student self-evaluation. You can give self-scoring quizzes. You can use special student-response sheets that reveal the correct answer when the appropriate spot is rubbed. And the computer is ideal as a self-evaluation tool; it provides instant feedback and effective follow-up.

Using Evaluation for Recording and Reporting Purposes

The final purpose of evaluation is the two-fold one of recording and reporting progress. This purpose is usually accomplished through tests administered at several decision points: the end of a unit, the end of a marking period, the end of a term, the end of a school year, or the end of a multi-year period.

The results of such tests are used for several purposes: to inform parents about student progress and achievement; to inform students about progress and achievement; to assist teachers and administrators in making decisions about group placement, summer school placement, and promotion; and to establish eligibility for prizes and awards.

When such tests are administered at the end of a unit, the results can also be used for instructional purposes: you can determine which skills and concepts need re-teaching before proceeding to the next unit.

Developing valid and reliable classroom tests is an important and complex skill, usually emphasized in courses on tests and measurements. Its complexity is exemplified in a 17-step flowchart developed by Nitko (1983) that shows all the steps that should be taken by test-makers in developing a valid achievement test.

While the process he describes is useful in developing major departmental examinations that have major impact on the student's educational future, it is perhaps too complex and time-consuming for making classroom unit tests. What follows, then, is a simplified process that will result in better tests.

The first step is to assess the constraints and resources: What constraints, such as time and student attention span, will place limits on the nature of the test? What resources, such as teachers' guides to textbooks, are available to help develop the test?

The second step is to analyze what was taught. There are two useful ways of doing this. Berliner (1987) recommends that the teacher develop a two-dimensional matrix for the analysis. Down the left-hand side, the teacher lists the content areas. For example, the content areas for a unit on the Civil War might include these: causes of the war, alignment of states in the war, significant battles in the war, people who played key roles in the war, and results of the war. Across the top, the matrix classifies the desired behaviors of students. Berliner uses three classifications: knowledge/comprehension, application, and analysis/synthesis/application. The teacher then uses the matrix to identify foci for test items. Thus, the intersection of the content area of *people who played key roles* with the desired behavior of *analysis/synthesis/evalaution* would yield this focus for a test item:

Evaluate Lee and Grant in relation to their effectiveness as generals.

An alternative method is illustrated in Figure 8-2. This method uses categories of objectives that seem more in keeping with the way teachers conceptualize units. The categories are: terms, facts and information, major concepts, skills and processes, and critical thinking and problem-solving skills. The method serves the same purpose as the content/behavior matrix; it simply uses different categories.

The unit analysis form can be distributed to students to help them prepare for the test; it can also be used by the teacher as a means of guiding the review work.

Next, determine which objectives will be tested. You select from the complete list those items that you believe should be tested, considering such elements as the importance of that item for future work, the amount of time devoted to teaching it, the resources available, and the time required for testing it.

You can record these decisions either by simply circling the tested areas on the unit analysis form, or you can construct another chart like the one shown in Figure 8-3.

The fourth step is to determine relative weights for all objectives to be tested. The weights serve three purposes: they help the teacher prepare the test; they help the student allocate time during the test; and they aid the teacher in scoring the test. The easiest way to indicate relative weights is with percentage figures as demonstrated in Figure 8-3.

Next, write the test items, using the information shown in Figure 8-3. First, determine the type of questions to be used for each objective, weighing both issues of validity (Which type will most validly assess learning?) and utility (Which type will be easiest to score?)

Figure 8-2
UNIT ANALYSIS FORM

Topic: Environmental Awareness

1. List the terms taught.

   Natural resource, renewable resource, pollution, environment, conservation, water-treatment plant, sewage-treatment plant, phosphate, algae, solar energy

2. List the facts and information taught.

   - The Environmental Protection Agency is a government agency that monitors compliance with laws.
   - Taking a shower uses 95 liters of water; taking a bath uses 133 liters.
   - The manufacture of plastics requires the use of strong chemicals and high temperatures.
   - Between 1980 and 1985, the world population increased by about 550 million people.

3. List the major concepts taught.

   - The water cycle
   - Acid rain

4. List the skills and processes taught.

   - Students can interpret a table of data.
   - Students can identify common causes of air pollution.

5. List the critical thinking and problem-solving objectives taught.

   - Students can analyze the trade-off involved in requiring factories to reduce pollution.
   - Students can explain how one person can make a difference in conservation.

Figure 8-3
OBJECTIVES TO BE TAUGHT

OBJECTIVE	WEIGHT
Terms	
Renewable resource, conservation, phos-phate, algae, solar energy	10%
Facts and Information	
None	0%
Major Concepts	
Water cycle	15%
Acid rain	15%
Skills and Processes	
Interpret table of data.	15%
Identify common causes of air pollution.	10%
Critical Thinking and Problem Solving	
Analyze trade-offs, clean air, fewer jobs.	15%
Explain how you can make a difference.	20%

When it comes to question types, you have several choices: essay question, fill-in-the-blank or supply-the-answer, true-false, matching, multiple choice, and performance or demonstration. Each of these has its own advantages and limitations. Essay questions best tap the ability to reason, but are difficult to score. Fill-in-the-blank or supply-the-answer are best for sampling knowledge, but are a bit more time-consuming than other short-answer types—both for the student and the teacher. True-false are easy to score—but permit guessing and also do not validly assess many objectives that cannot be so dichotomized. Matching and multiple-choice are useful short-answer types, but again, involve a guessing factor. As explained more fully later, performance tests probably yield more valid information about learning, but are difficult to construct and score.

After deciding question types, you are ready to write the questions and assemble the test. In assembling the test, you have several choices about how questions should be ordered and grouped. You can group by content; for example, all the questions dealing with the battles of the Civil War could be grouped together. You can group by behavior desired, grouping all the knowledge-comprehension items together. As Bloom, Hastings, and Madaus recommend when the items are relatively homogeneous with respect to content and behavior, you can group by difficulty, beginning with the easier questions. Or, when you use an assortment of question types (such as true-false and multiple choice), you can group by type. Doing so makes it easier for the teacher to give directions and the student to follow them.

The final step is to write clear directions. Use simple language that the students can read and understand. Write full directions; do not rely on the explanations you might give orally when you administer the test. And indicate the point value.

Now you are ready to review and revise the test. Give the test to a colleague and ask him or her to identify any potential problems. Review the test yourself to be sure that the directions are clear. As a final check, take the test yourself to check on the time required and the clarity of directions.

Evaluating by Assessing Performance

Because of growing dissatisfaction with paper-and-pencil tests, educators are increasingly exploring the use of performance, exhibition, or demonstration assessment, in which the student is asked to perform or demonstrate competence. Such performance or demonstration measures are typically recommended for evaluation at the end of some level of schooling, such as middle or high school.

Sizer (1984) believes that a high school diploma should be awarded on the basis of what he terms an "exhibition of mastery," which requires the student to demonstrate real intellectual accomplishments. Such exhibitions, as he describes them, would be public performances at which the student would prove that he or she had mastered certain broad skills and knowledge bases.

Here, for example, is a performance test that could be used in grades K–4 in mathematics. Students are given a large box of raisins and asked to estimate the number of raisins in it. To accomplish the task, they are provided with a balance, containers of different sizes, and a calculator. They must use a second method to check their first estimate and record the results. (This test was cited by Mitchell 1992, as based on the standards of the National Council of Teachers of Mathematics.)

Wiggins (1989) identifies eight intellectual design features of such demonstrations: (1) they are essential (not just for a grade); (2) they are enabling (point the learner toward more complex use of skills); (3) they are contextualized and complex (not discrete skills taken out of context); (4) they involve student research; (5) they assess habits and repertoires (not recall or "plug-in" skills); (6) they are representative (emphasizing depth, not breadth); (7) they are engaging and educational; and (8) they involve ambiguous tasks to reflect life's ambiguities.

While the art of developing demonstrations or performance measures is a relatively recent one, some preliminary writings in the field suggest that a process like the following would be used. (For a fuller discussion of the process, see Archibald and Newman 1988 and Stiggins 1988.)

The initial step is to identify a major educational goal you want the student to achieve at the end of a certain level of schooling. The goal should be a general one that encompasses several component skills and knowledge bases; it should also have educational significance. Suppose, for example, that you wanted all eighth graders to have achieved this goal: Become a more discriminating and critical user of television.

Your next action would be to analyze that goal into its constituent behaviors—the more specific behaviors that constitute the general goal. This second step will help you develop the demonstration measures. As you complete this second step, keep in mind both the developmental level of the learners and the limits of what is attainable in schooling.

Here, for example, are the constituent behaviors that might be identified for our general eighth grade goal:

- Limit television viewing to not more than 12 hours a week.
- Use selection tools (such as critics' columns and newspaper schedules) to identify important shows to watch.
- Demonstrate an awareness of how commercials attempt to shape behavior by appealing to basic human drives and needs.
- Evaluate television news shows for objectivity and fairness.

Now you should identify the demonstrations or performances required for the student to exhibit mastery. Wiggins (1989) suggests seven structural features here: (1) involve the public; (2) do not rely on arbitrary time constraints; (3) offer known tasks;

(4) offer tasks that recur in life and are worth practicing; (5) require cumulative evidence of performance, such as a portfolio; (6) require collaboration; and (7) make feedback central.

Here are the demonstrations or performances that the teachers might require for the critical viewing goal we identified:

1. You are to present to the class two logs of television viewing: one showing your viewing schedule at the beginning of the school year; the second showing your viewing schedule at the end of the school year. You will explain to the class the major differences between the two logs.

2. You and four of your classmates will be given a copy of the entertainment section of the Sunday newspaper and a copy of *Newsweek* magazine for the coming week. You will be expected to identify five shows that you consider important to watch and explain why you have chosen them.

3. You will be shown videotapes of three commercials for a popular brand of athletic shoes. You will explain in a well-written essay how those commercials are attempting to influence your buying behavior.

The final step is to devise a scoring plan that you will use in evaluating the performance, including the score-recording method to be used. Stiggins (1987) identifies these score recording methods as possibilities: checklist, rating scale, anecdotal record, portfolio, audio or video tape.

While some have questioned the practicality of such complex performance measures, they do seem to be a very promising alternative to paper-and-pencil objective tests.

EVALUATION OF TEACHERS

Teacher evaluation is a key part of the entire evaluation program. While there is not much that you can do on your own, you can do a great deal in working with colleagues to design and implement a more productive evaluation system.

In discussing teacher evaluation, it would be useful first to make a distinction between two terms that will be used here to denote two different approaches. First, *rating* is a process of assigning scores or grades (such as *satisfactory* or *unsatisfactory*) to teachers for purposes of administrative decision-making. In this sense, the principal rates teachers to make decisions about such matters as tenure, contract renewal, and promotion. Rating serves an accountability purpose.

This rating process is contrasted with *evaluation*, which is used here to mean a process of assessing performance as a means of fostering growth. Periodically, like all committed professionals, you assess your teaching to determine if there are any "craft" skills you need to refine or any of the "science" skills you need to develop. Evaluation has a growth orientation.

As Stiggins and Duke (1988) note, the two processes should be kept distinct. The rating process does not improve instruction, despite the claims of those who make the assertion. And the evaluation process, as the term is used here, is not an adequate basis for making such decisions as denying tenure or awarding merit pay.

Making Rating More Effective for Probationary Teachers and Tenured Teachers

Establishing the procedures for the rating process should be the task of a district committee composed of administrators, supervisors, and classroom teachers. They should systematically deal with the following issues:

Who Should Be Rated?

Two groups of teachers should be rated each year: all probationary teachers and any tenured teacher who is experiencing serious difficulty. Identifying the first group is easy enough; identifying the second requires some systematic work. You and your colleagues should cooperate with the principal (and with district administrators) in developing procedures by which the principal can recommend any marginally competent tenured teacher for the rating track. The decision to place a tenured teacher on the rating track should be made very deliberately and should use multiple observations and data sources. It would also be important to provide due-process procedures for the teacher to appeal this decision.

What Criteria Should Be Used?

The committee should develop clear and specific criteria that are based upon the craft of teaching—the essential basics of effective teaching. Those criteria should also encompass the administrative responsibilities assigned to the teacher.

What Data Sources Should Be Used?

Multiple data sources should be used: results of classroom observations, self-appraisals, lesson plans, grade and record books, teacher-made tests. Note that I do not recommend using students' test results to rate teachers. Because there are so many factors that teachers cannot control, it is not fair to hold them accountable for student learning.

Who Should Do the Rating?

In most schools the principal does the rating. However, many school systems have found that external evaluators can be more objective. And in some school systems, teachers have taken over the rating process, with very positive results (Pfeifer 1987). The role of the rater is not as important as ensuring that there are multiple raters and that all raters have been trained and evaluated. (Someone noted this irony: It takes about 12 years of study to become a judge of cattle; it takes only one course in supervision to become a judge of teaching.)

Obviously, this rating process is an intensive, time-consuming task. However, it is an important one. If we really want to improve our profession, then we have to find better ways of removing incompetent teachers.

Making Evaluation More Productive
For All Other Teachers

All the rest of the faculty should be involved in evaluation, not rating. The following attributes are the key components of a productive evaluation system.

- *It focuses on growth.* There are no scorecards, rating forms, or evaluation instruments.

- *It is goal-oriented.* Teachers are given special training in setting for themselves one or two significant growth goals. Duke (1990) notes that this goal-setting process is so crucial and so difficult that teachers should participate in an intensive pre-goal setting stage in which they receive special training and practice in setting meaningful goals.

- *It emphasizes self-appraisal.* A significant part of the process requires the teacher to make a self-appraisal.

- *The paperwork is minimal.* Too many goal-based systems are so complicated that they become a burden.

- *While it is ongoing for all teachers, it is formalized only once every four years.* This minimizes the work involved for teachers and administrators.

- *It is peer-directed.* The teachers take charge. The administrators are needed only to facilitate and monitor the system.

- *It uses multiple data sources.* These sources are reported in a portfolio.

- *It is adequately supported.* It is supported with the necessary staff development and other resources needed.

The following description is one way that such a system might work. (The system described below encompasses and builds upon the recommendations of Darling-Hammond 1990.) First, all the competent experienced teachers are divided into four

144

cohorts—A, B, C, and D. Cohort A goes through the formal evaluation process the first year; Cohort B, the second; and so on. All teachers are given the requisite training in self-appraisal and goal setting. While the teachers in one cohort are participating in the formal process, the rest of the tenured teachers are left on their own, trusted to develop as they see the need to grow.

During the year that a cohort is formally evaluated, each teacher involved begins with a self-appraisal, one that focuses on the science of teaching or that draws from the school-improvement plan. For example, a mathematics teacher might use the research on teaching mathematics to assess his or her current level of achievement. As a result of that appraisal, the teacher sets one significant growth goal. Here is an example:

> During this school year the students in my classes will become more effective in solving mathematical problems.

Note that the goal is set in terms of student learning, not teacher behavior. Then the teacher indicates what he or she will do to accomplish that goal. Here are some strategies that would be effective with the goal above: Review the research on mathematical problem-solving; attend a workshop on mathematical problem-solving; confer with colleagues who are also working on problem-solving; plan and implement special lessons on problem-solving, with a colleague observing and giving feedback; developing better assessment methods for problem-solving.

The teacher then implements that growth plan. At the end of the year, the teacher presents to colleagues and administrators a portfolio that includes the evidence of accomplishment. In this instance, the portfolio might include the following: summary of research, report on workshop attended, summary of conferences with colleagues, special lesson plans on problem-solving, video tape of problem-solving lesson, sample of assessment method for evaluating problem solving.

Obviously, each school system would develop its own plan. Some might wish to place more emphasis on collegial teams and a team proposal; some might wish to use the formal evaluation every three or five years; some might simplify the entire process so that it is less time-consuming.

FOR FURTHER READING

Macphail-Wilcox, B. and Forbes, R. 1990. *Administrator evaluation handbook.* Bloomington, Ind.: Phi Delta Kappa. One of the best handbooks available on evaluating administrators.

Millman, J. and Darling-Hammond, L. 1990. *The new handbook of teacher evaluation.* Newbury Park, Calif.: Sage. Includes several very useful chapters on the processes and issues in teacher evaluation.

Raupp, M. 1990. *Evaluation management handbook.* Andover, Mass.: The Network. A clear and practical guide to designing program evaluations.

REFERENCES

Archibald, D. and Newmann, F. 1988. *Beyond standardized testing: Authentic academic achievement in the secondary school.* Reston, Vir.: National Association of Secondary School Principals.

Berliner, D.C. 1987. But do they understand? In *Educator's handbook. A research perspective,* ed. V. Richardson-Koehler, 259–94. New York: Longman.

Bloom, B.S.; Hastings, J.T.; and Madaus, G.F. 1971. *Handbook on formative and summative evaluation of student learning.* New York: McGraw-Hill.

Butler, J. 1987. *Homework.* Portland, Ore.: Northwest Regional Educational Laboratory School Improvement Program.

Curry, L. 1990. A critique of the research on learning styles. *Educational Leadership,* 48(2): 50–6.

Darling-Hammond, L. 1990. Teacher evaluation in transition: Emerging roles and evolving methods. In *The new handbook of teacher evaluation*, eds. J. Millman and L. Darling-Hammond, 17–34. Newbury Park, Calif.: Sage.

Duke, D.L. 1990. Setting goals for professional development. *Educational Leadership*, 47(8): 71–5.

Dunn, R. and Griggs, S.A. 1988. *Learning styles: Quiet revolution in American secondary schools*. Reston, Vir.: National Association of Secondary School Principals.

Dunn, R.; Beaudry, J.S.; and Klavas, A. 1989. Survey of research on learning styles. *Educational Leadership*, 47(6): 50–8.

Glatthorn, A.A. 1991. Secondary English classroom environments. In *Handbook of research on teaching the English language arts;* eds. J. Flood; J.M. Jensen; D. Lapp; J.R. Squire; 438–56. New York: Macmillan.

Good, T.L. and Brophy, J.E. 1987. *Looking in classrooms*, 4th ed. New York: Harper and Row.

Guild, P.B. and Garger, S. 1985. *Marching to different drummers*. Alexander, Vir.: Association for Supervision and Curriculum Development.

Guskey, T.R. 1985. *Implementing mastery learning*. Belmont, Calif.: Wadsworth.

Hallinan, M.T. and Sorenson, A.B. 1983. The formation and stability of instructional groups. *American Sociological Review*, vol. 48, 838–51.

Mitchell, R. 1992. *Testing for learning: How new approaches to evaluation can improve American schools*. New York: Free Press.

Nitko, A. 1983. *Educational tests and measurements: An introduction*. Orlando, Fla.: Harcourt Brace Jovanovich.

Pfeifer, R.S. 1987. *Variations on a theme: An analysis of peer involvement in teacher evaluation*. Paper presented at annual meeting of the

American Educational Research Association, Washington, D.C.

Sizer, T. 1984. *Horace's compromise: The dilemma of the American high school.* Boston: Houghton Mifflin.

Stiggins, R.J. 1987. *Measuring thinking skills through classroom assessment.* Portland, Ore.: Northwest Regional Educational Laboratory.

Stiggins, R.J. and Duke, D. 1988. *The case for commitment to teacher growth.* Albany, N.Y.: State University of New York Press.

Wiggins, G. 1989. Teaching to the (authentic) test. *Educational Leadership,* 46(7): 41–7.

Chapter 9

FOUNDATION ELEMENTS: CULTURE, CLIMATE, AND RELATED COMPONENTS

The *foundation elements* make up the culture, the climate, and other related elements of a school. They are like the foundation of a house; they provide the support for all that grows from them. The first section of this chapter identifies and explains these elements. The second section discusses their implications for you and your colleagues.

THE NATURE OF THE FOUNDATION ELEMENTS

Figure 9-1 shows how the foundation elements are related. The diagram will be used as the organizational basis for this section.

The Culture

The most important foundation element is the *culture* of the school. Variously defined, it is perhaps best understood as Schein (1985) defines it: the system of shared meanings, assumptions, and underlying values of an organization. And of these three elements, the core values seem most fundamental. To understand the importance of values, think about how many of the values listed in Chapter 3 (Figure 3-4) are shared by your administrator and your colleagues. The values of a school are sometimes stated as a philosophy. Here, for example, is how the first value of "democracy"(listed in Figure 3-4) might appear in a statement of a school's philosophy:

We believe in democracy. We share power with all those involved, within the limits of their maturity. All those affected by decisions have a voice in making those decisions.

149

Figure 9-1. The Foundation Elements

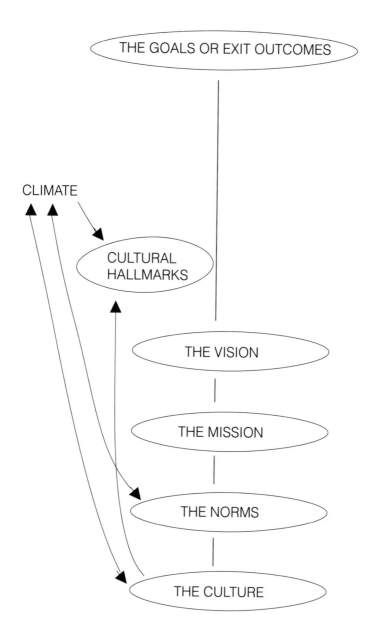

Your school's culture is expressed in the hidden curriculum and pervades almost every aspect of school life. Obviously, it is critically important.

The Climate

If those core values are held by administrators and teachers, then all else follows. To begin with, they help create and are in turn influenced by the climate. *Climate*, another slippery term, is used here in the way specified by Reichers and Schneider (1990) as: "the shared perception of the way things are here" (p. 22). It is the shared perceptions that you and all others in the school have about the policies, practices, and procedures of the school. As the diagram suggests, climate is the all-encompassing "weather" that makes the organization attractive or unattractive to members.

The following aspects of a desirable school climate have been identified from a review of the literature on school climate. They are also presented here as a statement that might be adopted by a school faculty.

This is what we want our school to be like:

1. *Safe and orderly.* Learning takes place best when people feel safe and where there is a sense of order.

2. *Considerate and caring.* Learning is at its best when people feel they are cared for.

3. *Optimistic and forward-looking.* Schools are better places to learn and work when people feel hopeful, have high morale, and work toward a brighter future.

4. *Respectful and trusting.* Schools are better when people respect and trust each other.

5. *Collaborative and cooperative.* Goals are better accomplished when people work together.

6. *Productive and growth-oriented.* We are here to learn and grow.

151

(For the research on the attributes and importance of school climate, see: Fox 1974, O'Neal et al. 1987, and Smith and Piele 1989.)

As Sergiovanni (1987) notes, a positive school climate does not guarantee school effectiveness, but it is a necessary ingredient of effective schools.

Norms

The culture and climate together produce the *norms*—the standards of behavior to which people conform. In everyday language, the norms are "the way we do things here." The norms are often unstated, until they are violated. This implicit nature often makes it difficult for teachers new to a school to understand what the norms are.

Here are the norms usually considered desirable, again stated as faculty members might state them for themselves and the students:

- *We work hard.* Teachers don't run out of the building before the students. Students don't "goof off."

- *We cooperate.* We don't compete with each other or hoard materials. The only enemy is ignorance.

- *We are honest.* We don't manipulate others, ignore problems, or conceal important information that should be shared.

- *We trust each other.* We don't check up on each other unduly or watch each other closely to catch mistakes.

- *We take sensible chances.* We value innovation and improvement, and we know that improvement involves risk-taking.

- *We give everybody an equal opportunity.* We don't discriminate or show favorites. Ethnicity, age, gender, social class do not matter to us.

- *We learn and grow.* We realize that we don't have all the answers. We want to grow because it is self-satisfying, not because we are forced to grow.

152

(For the research on both the positive and negative effects of such norms, see: Cusick 1992; McLaughlin and Yee 1988; Powell, Farrar, and Cohen 1985.)

Obviously, such norms cannot be imposed, but they can be articulated, reinforced, and rewarded.

Cultural Hallmarks

The underlying culture, the organizational climate, and the norms of behavior all impact upon and give rise to *cultural hallmarks*, the visible expressions of those underlying elements. The hallmarks usually cited in the literature are the following:

- *The heroes.* Great leaders of the past are remembered.
- *The myths.* The stories of great events, such as "the time we won the championship," are retold, usually in an embellished form.
- *The stories.* School members tell again and again the same stories about the school's past.
- *The rituals and ceremonies.* Celebrations, such as a winter festival and a spring tree-planting, are ongoing activities that unite the school.
- *Symbols.* Symbols, such as a mascot and a slogan, represent the school's character and aspirations.

(For a discussion of cultural manifestations, see Deal and Kennedy 1982.)

While much has been made of such manifestations, it is helpful to remember that these are only the surface manifestations. Some leaders have foolishly believed that they can change the culture by installing new ceremonies or devising new slogans. Common sense would tell you that to do so is like painting the siding of the house when the foundation is falling apart.

The Mission

Sharing important values in a supportive school climate leads to a shared sense of *mission*—a common belief in the central purpose of the school. The mission of a school is usually articulated in a *mission statement,* which sets forth the unique purpose of that school. As Ackoff (1987) observes, the mission statement does not have to be immediately implementable, only desirable.

Here is an example of a mission statement, produced by the teachers and administrators of Prince William County (Virginia) schools:

> Our mission is to provide a high quality, comprehensive, and relevant education to all students. In our schools each student will experience success. Each student will be treated as an individual, empowered as a learner, and taught to function effectively as a member of a group. (H.E. Burkett, personal communication, February 17, 1992.)

This particular mission statement was produced through a great deal of discussion among and involvement of all faculty members. That process is even more important than the product. Too many educators misunderstand that relationship. Consider these two scenarios:

Scenario 1:

Hobart Thomas, principal of Jones Middle School, runs a tight ship with a very authoritarian hand. He goes to a school-improvement workshop, where he hears that mission statements are very important. In response, he writes one, by following a model he received at the workshop. He includes something about *collegiality,* because he heard that it is the current buzz word. He then asks teachers to revise and endorse the mission statement. Because these teachers have grown used to his authoritarian style, they rubber-stamp it. Thomas is convinced that his school has accomplished something significant.

Scenario 2:

Through dynamic leadership and hard work, Michelle Davis, the principal of a rural school that serves poor families, has selected and developed a faculty who all share the same values. Faculty members work together in creating a climate of caring and cooperation. They operationalize their values in an exciting and challenging program. They all have a very clear idea of what their central purpose is—they want to broaden the horizons of these poor children and empower them to change their futures. They are all so busy that they have just never taken the time to write a mission statement.

Which is likely to be the more effective school? Obviously, the school described in Scenario 2 is the one. It is not the mission statement that matters. It is instead the fact that all those involved in making the school work have a very clear understanding of why the school exists, what their ultimate purpose is, and how they are different from other schools.

Vision

The mission is often reflected in a *vision*. The vision is your dream of what the school can be. You know the power of visions. Think about Martin Luther King, Jr.'s famous "I have a dream..." speech. The vision lifts our eyes from the real ground before us to the horizon of possibilities.

There are several important cautions, however, about such visions. The first three involve visions produced by charismatic leaders and transmitted to "followers." A vision conceived by one person is often quite specific or narrow. As Fullan (1992) points out, such a vision can be blinding in several ways. A narrow vision that focuses on a single component (such as cooperative learning) can be limiting. Here, the words of Louis and Miles (1990) are so apposite that they need to be quoted: "The more narrow and specific the objectives of external programs that stimulate the improvement effort, the more likely the school is to run into problems in creating its own vision for school reform" (p. 225).

A vision produced by a charismatic principal depends too much on the single leader for its actualization; when that principal leaves, things fall apart. Finally, a vision promulgated and espoused by one leader can reduce the leader's opportunities for growth because other visions typically are excluded.

The second caution about visions is that they require several preconditions, as explained by Louis and Miles (1990). First, the school needs a visionary principal, who can develop in teachers the capacity to dream big. Second, there needs to be reasonable staff cohesiveness—a spirit among the staff of togetherness, affiliation, and oneness. Third, there needs to be school-based control over staffing. If the principal and the teachers cannot control who joins them, it becomes very difficult to maintain a shared vision. These scholars also point out rather astutely that a vision is generated out of the planning process, rather than prior to it. You and your colleagues work with the principal to identify and solve problems; then you think about what vision has been driving you.

Here is the vision statement developed by the same Maryland school system that developed the mission statement, again through a systematic process of discussion and involvement.

In the Prince William County Public Schools all students will learn to their fullest capacity. The education of each student will be individualized and developmentally appropriate. Student learning will be facilitated by using national, global, and multicultural perspectives. Students who graduate from Prince William County Schools will possess knowledge and skills that will assure their proficiency in problem-solving and the use of technology. Graduates will have a love of learning and the skills to be lifelong learners. They will be morally and socially responsible citizens. All graduates will be competent to enter the work world and be prepared to pursue advanced educational opportunities.

Such a vision statement helps all involved keep their eyes on a bright future.

Goals

The final foundation element is a set of shared goals. The *goals* are the specific ends the school wants to accomplish for all students, through all aspects of the program. Those espousing "outcomes-based education," call them *exit outcomes*. (See Spady 1988, for an explanation of the salient features of outcomes-based education and the importance of exit outcomes.) Such goals are often produced by state departments of education and then transmitted to school systems for implementation. One useful formulation of goals that you and your colleagues might review is that provided by Goodlad (1984).

If your school district does not have a clear set of educational goals, then you and your colleagues should cooperate with your principal to generate your school's goals. Those school goals can then be used to develop program goals (such as the goals for mathematics or science), course goals (such as the goals for algebra or biology), and unit and lesson outcomes. Such a tightly articulated set of outcomes seems generally more effective than goals that are only loosely joined with each other. In thinking about goal statements, keep in mind again the admonition about form versus substance. What matters is that you and your colleagues have achieved a strong consensus about the major goals you are trying to achieve. The verbal formulation is much less crucial.

THE IMPLICATIONS FOR YOU
AND YOUR COLLEAGUES

What do you do if you suspect the foundations are shaky? That's a rather complicated issue. Chapter 11 details a comprehensive change process that can be used in making any complex change. Let's close this chapter with some guidelines for changing the foundations and some suggestions for a specific change strategy as it relates to these elements. (The guidelines have been derived from the literature on organizational change, especially the following: Block 1987; Louis and Miles 1990; Smith and Piele 1989.)

Guidelines in Strengthening the Foundations

In strengthening the foundations, keep these guidelines in mind:

- *Recognize that words matter.* People listen to what you say. If you talk in the departmental office about sports and fashions, that makes one impression. If you talk about the school's mission and your educational values, that says something quite different. If you publish and send to parents only information about fund-raising activities, your school creates a different impression than one that publishes and distributes its vision.

- *Solve problems.* Actions matter even more than words. Focus on solving major problems. Schools improve through concerted action.

- *Work together and share the credit.* The mythic charismatic principal who singlehandedly "turned the school around" in two years is good for television and films, but it isn't the way real schools achieve lasting improvement. Collegiality and cooperation result in sustained change, not dramatic fixes that last only as long as the principal lasts.

- *Work on the basics.* Focus on what really matters—your values, your sense of shared purpose, your vision of what the school can be. The surface elements—the slogans, the symbols, and the rituals—can come later.

- *Be patient.* Change is always complicated; complex educational change is perhaps the most complicated of all. There are no quick fixes. And try not to evaluate new programs prematurely.

- *Train.* Uninformed and unskilled people can't bring about meaningful improvements. Everyone needs the kind of staff development described in Chapter 4.

- *Think—before, during, and after you act.* The "reflective professional" is more than a slogan—it's what the profession is all about.

A Strategy for Strengthening the Foundation

Each school, of course, must develop its own strategy for strengthening the foundation elements. What follows is a general approach, derived from the literature on organizational change and my own experience.

Begin with action, focusing on one specific foundation element. You and your colleagues might consider initially zeroing in on the climate. There are several reasons for focusing on the climate. It is a critical element; it is easily measured; and it is susceptible to specific interventions. A special or existing faculty committee can start by building its knowledge base, especially looking for valid and reliable measures of climate. The best source here is the work by Gottfredson et al. (1986).

The committee can then follow a change strategy recommended by O'Neal and her colleagues (1987). First, review the data to identify areas in need of improvement. For each area, identify specific goals. Then develop a plan for improving within that specific area. Next, implement the plan and evaluate its effects. Finally, begin the process all over again when the need arises.

The hope is that the work of this committee will create a sense of momentum and get faculty and administrators working together in a cooperative mode. Then, as the climate committee completes its work, organize a second committee to work with the faculty in developing student goals. The student goals can become the basis for improving the curriculum and the assessment process.

Once again, the committee should start by building the knowledge base, reviewing the goals as set forth by Goodlad (1984), examining goals developed by the state and the school district, and reviewing the literature on the changing society and its educational needs. In this process of goal-setting, the committee should work for the comprehensive involvement of all constituencies—administrators, teachers, students, parents, and civic and business leaders.

With those two foundation projects nearly completed or underway, you and your colleagues should next consider drafting a statement of your philosophy. Doing so will give you a good opportunity to examine the values shared by the entire faculty. Don't rush this task. Explain the importance of it and provide plenty of opportunity for faculty input.

Now, examine the cultural hallmarks. Again, a special faculty committee can assess the present hallmarks and determine what additional hallmarks it might introduce in a natural manner. Do you need more celebrations? Do you need a new slogan or symbol?

All this time the culture has been changing gradually. You are acting collaboratively to improve the climate. You have clarified your goals. You have discussed openly the values that motivate you. And the norms have been changing without special pronouncements. People are acting differently because they feel they are part of an improving organization. At this stage, you may now turn your attention to the writing of your mission and vision statements.

This is not a rational, linear process. But schools are nonrational organizations, where a broken-front change strategy seems more effective. Finally, keep in mind that changing the foundation elements are complex, time-consuming matters. Changing the schedule will take you a few weeks. Changing the culture will require a few years.

FOR FURTHER READING

Joyce, B. 1990. *Changing school culture through staff development.* Alexandria, Vir.: Association for Supervision and Curriculum Development. Several excellent chapters on the importance of staff development in changing the culture.

Lieberman, A. 1990. *Schools as collaborative culture: Creating the future now.* New York: Falmer. A comprehensive analysis of the need for a collaborative culture—and how to achieve it.

Louis, K.S. and Miles, M.B. 1990. *Improving the urban high school: What works and why.* New York: Teachers College Press. This excellent text is broader than its title suggests. It offers tested methods for improving all schools.

REFERENCES

Ackoff, R.L. 1987. Mission statements. *Planning Review,* 15: 30–1.

Block, P. 1987. *The empowered manager: Positive political skills at work.* San Francisco: Jossey Bass.

Cusick, P.A. 1992. *The educational system: Its nature and logic.* New York: McGraw-Hill.

Deal, T.E. and Kennedy, A.A. 1982. *Corporate cultures: The rites and rituals of organized life.* Reading, Mass.: Addison-Wesley.

Fox, R.S. 1974. *School climate improvement: A challenge to the school administrator.* Bloomington, Ind.: Phi Delta Kappa.

Fullan, M.G. 1992. Visions that blind. *Educational Leadership,* 49(5): 19–20.

Goodlad, J.I. 1984. *A place called school: Prospects for the future.* New York: McGraw-Hill.

Gottfredson, D.C., et al. 1986. *School climate assessment instruments: A review.* Baltimore, Md.: Center for Social Organization of Schools, Johns Hopkins University. ERIC Document Reproduction Service # ED 278 702.

Louis, K.S. and Miles, M.B. 1990. *Improving the urban high school: What works and why.* New York: Teachers College Press.

McLaughlin, M.W. and Yee, S.M. 1988. School as a place to have a career. In *Building a professional culture*, ed. A.A. Lieberman, 23–44. New York: Teachers College Press.

O'Neal, D.H.; O'Neal, M.S.; Short, M.L.; Holmes, C.T.; Brown, C.L.; DeWeese, L.S.; and Careter, M. 1987. *Improving school climate.* Athens, Ga.: Bureau of Educational Services, University of Georgia.

Powell, A.G.; Farrar, E.; and Cohen, D.K. 1985. *The shopping mall high school.* Boston: Houghton Mifflin.

Reichers, A.E. and Schneider, B. 1990. Climate and culture: An evolution of constructs. In *Organizational climate and culture*, ed. I.L. Goldstein, 5–39. San Francisco: Jossey Bass.

Schein, E. 1985. *Organizational culture and leadership: A dynamic view.* San Francisco: Jossey Bass.

Sergiovanni, T.J. 1987. *The principalship: A reflective practice perspective.* Newton, Mass.: Allyn and Bacon.

Smith, S.C. and Piele, P.K. 1989. *School leadership: Handbook for excellence.* 2d ed. Eugene, Ore.: ERIC Clearinghouse on Educational Management, University of Oregon.

Spady, W.G. 1988. Organizing for results: The basis for authentic restructuring and reform. *Educational Leadership*, 46(2): 4–8.

Chapter 10

COLLEGIAL LEADERSHIP

During the past several years, a marked shift has occurred in our thinking about school leadership. Previous to that, the focus was on the principal as an instructional leader. Researchers systematically studied what principals did in effective schools, deriving checklists that enumerated behaviors such as "monitors the curriculum." Then something interesting happened. Leaders in the field re-discovered the theories of James McGregor Burns (1978), who in the 1970s wrote a book about "transformational leadership," and the theories of W. Edwards Deming (1988), the management consultant who went to Japan in the 1950s to teach the Japanese how to produce high quality goods and services. Field leaders also discovered the power of teams and the importance of collegiality. Now the rhetoric has shifted. The talk is of "transformational leadership," "total quality management," and "team leadership."

While it would be easy to ridicule the researchers and leaders who were so slow to discover these visionaries and their powerful ideas, it would make more sense to analyze this shift in thinking and determine its implications for you as a classroom teacher. This chapter, then, focuses on three related issues. It first provides a closer analysis of this new perspective on leadership. It then looks closely at two mechanisms by which it is implemented in schools: school-based management and team leadership.

THE NEW APPROACH TO LEADERSHIP

The chief contrasts between the old perspective, termed here the *traditional* approach, and the new perspective, identified as the *transformational* approach, are summarized in Figure 10-1 and discussed as follows. (The discussion draws primarily from these sources: Burns 1978, Deming 1988, Leithwood 1992, and Sergiovanni 1992.)

Figure 10-1
ANALYSIS OF LEADERSHIP PERSPECTIVES

COMPONENT/ TYPE	TRADITIONAL	TRANSFORMA-TIONAL
Focus	Improving effective-ness by accomplish-ing tasks	Achieving excel-lence by transform-ing the culture
Leadership Structure	Principal as leader	Team leadership
Organizational Structure	Hierarchical Centralized	Learning community Decentralized
Source of Power	Role-based	Consensual
Decision Making	Unilateral	Participative
Improvement Process	Focus on specific goals	Focus on continuing development of people
Personnel Quality Desired	Technical competence	Moral commitment
Incentives	Important Use merit pay	Unimportant Transform people
Importance of Evaluation	Periodic inspections crucial	Build in quality Reduce inspections

1. *The focus is on achieving excellence by transforming the culture.* In the traditional approach, the main concern is increasing effectiveness by accomplishing tasks. Leaders are interested in incremental gains and achieve those modest gains by working toward specific tasks and goals. In the transformational approach, the concern is to achieve excellence by radically transforming the culture. The leaders move toward a vision of excellence by working constantly toward a transformation of the value structure. Leithwood (1992) makes the point that traditional leaders emphasize "first-order" changes, such as aligning the curriculum more closely. On the other hand, transformational leaders are concerned, he notes, with "second order" changes, such as building a shared vision.

2. *Leadership is perceived as functions performed by a team, not as a role discharged by a single individual.* The transformational approach stresses collegial or team leadership; it recognizes the fact that leadership includes processes that are most effectively used by cooperative teams to achieve common goals. All those with the needed knowledge and skills are expected to play a leadership role. In the traditional approach, the principal is seen as the active and sole leader, busily scurrying through the school, evaluating teachers and monitoring the curriculum. In a recent interview, Sergiovanni observed that an increase in teacher professionalism reduces the need for conventional leadership (Brandt 1992).

3. *The desired organizational structure is a learning community, with decentralized decision-making.* The old model of a hierarchical and bureaucratic organization with centralized decision-making is now seen as outmoded. In its place is the concept of a learning community, where people work together solving problems "on the line." In a learning community, all are vitally concerned with their own learning and the learning of those they work with and for. They cooperate, rather than compete. They share resources. They feel a shared concern about all those in the organization. They

165

give and receive feedback in a constructive manner because they are eager to learn.

4. *Power is consensual and facilitative, based on one's knowledge and skill, not on one's role.* Traditional leaders derive their power from several sources: their role ("I'm the principal"); their control of rewards and incentives ("Obey me, and you get a better schedule"); and their access to higher authority ("I have the ear of the superintendent"). Transformational leaders derive their power from quite different sources: their knowledge and skill in achieving group goals, their ability to energize others in accomplishing their shared vision, and their concern for those they serve. As the principal empowers teachers to take charge of their own professional growth, the power of the principal increases as he or she gains additional teacher support.

5. *The decision making is participative, not unilateral.* In the transformational approach, the major decisions are made through deliberation and participation of all involved and affected. Problems are identified by everyone on the team, not by the principal alone. Data are gathered by all those working on the problem. All participants share in generating solutions and responses. Rather than casting divisive votes, the group works toward building a consensus, ensuring that minority views are heard.

   There are two major exceptions to this participative consensual approach. First, in a crisis, the principal acts decisively, rather than appointing a committee. And the principal or assistant principal efficiently makes the decisions affecting the day-to-day operations of the school. Teachers do not want to be involved in deciding which custodian is responsible for the second floor or which vendor is chosen to repair the copying machine.

6. *The improvement process focuses on the continuing development of the people.* One of Deming's 14 principles is to institute a

vigorous program of education and self-improvement for everyone. If you and your colleagues work together to make yourselves better teachers, then you do not need to set such quantifiable goals as: "Eighty percent of my students will achieve 80 percent on the final examination." The school gets better because the people are stronger. The old "management-by-objectives" approach emphasized the importance of setting quantifiable goals and work quotas. As noted by Blankenstein (1992), there are several problems with numerical goals: (1) they are usually arbitrarily set; (2) setting quotas leads to marginal work; and (3) appraisal of individual performance based upon such specification of quantifiable goals is unfair and misguided.

7. *The main quality desired in people is moral commitment, or what Sergiovanni (1992) calls "professional virtue."* As he uses the concept, this virtue involves four commitments: a commitment to practice in an exemplary way; a commitment to practice toward valued social ends; a commitment not only to one's own practice, but to the practice itself; a commitment to the ethic of caring.

   To understand the critical importance of such commitment, consider two teachers. Teacher A has conscientiously mastered the "six-step lesson plan" because her principal put pressure on all the faculty to acquire those skills. However, Teacher A does not see the need for further development and gets defensive when consultants speak about alternative models of teaching. On the other hand, Teacher B never bothered with the details of the "six-step lesson plan" because she considered it too controlling. She continues to explore and acquire the advanced skills of teaching, never fully satisfied with her performance. She is committed to exemplary practice.

8. *Rather than using incentives to motivate better performance, the transformational leader transforms the aspirations of the people.* He or she knows that educators especially are driven by

167

internal forces to achieve the visions that energize them; they are not motivated by the promise of monetary rewards.

You can appreciate this distinction by thinking about what motivates you. If you are like most teachers, you work hard at school because you believe you can make a difference. You have a vision of what you can become as a teacher. You probably are working harder than you should. Would you work any harder if your school district promised you a $500 raise?

Because of his concern for quality people and team work, Deming considers merit pay a seriously flawed concept. It increases competition and takes the attention away from quality.

9. *The transformational leader builds in quality all along and spends little or no time in inspecting individual performance.* If you recruit and select the best teachers, and if you provide high quality staff development, then you do not need to worry about evaluating them. In his interview with Brandt, Sergiovanni was most direct on this point: "Evaluation systems aren't worth a nickel. They're one of the biggest wastes of time in the world" (pp.48–49).

The same principle applies to the curriculum. If you develop a high-quality curriculum with significant teacher input and give teachers the needed time, resources, and training, then you do not have to use excessive amounts of time in monitoring its implementation.

Obviously, it's important for you and your colleagues to examine and reflect upon these principles of the new leadership, not to accept them uncritically. One way to assess where you are and where you want to be is to construct a survey like the one shown in Figure 10-2. You should begin by holding some open discussions about what the principles mean and why they are important. Then administer the survey and summarize the results. You can analyze the results to determine where the greatest gap exists between what you

Figure 10-2
LEADERSHIP ASSESSMENT QUESTIONNAIRE

We would like your help in assessing the type of leadership our school has and the type it wants. We are concerned with structure and processes; we are not evaluating the principal. Consider each area of leadership. First indicate the actual situation by using one of these numbers to indicate where you think our school is right now. Then indicate the desired situation by using the same numbers.

CODE
1. Traditional
2. Mostly traditional but on the way to transformational
3. Getting close to transformational
4. Transformational

1. FOCUS
   Actual: 1   2   3   4
   Desired: 1   2   3   4
2. LEADERSHIP STRUCTURE
   Actual: 1   2   3   4
   Desired: 1   2   3   4
3. ORGANIZATIONAL STRUCTURE
   Actual: 1   2   3   4
   Desired: 1   2   3   4
4. SOURCE OF POWER
   Actual: 1   2   3   4
   Desired: 1   2   3   4
5. DECISION MAKING
   Actual: 1   2   3   4
   Desired: 1   2   3   4
6. IMPROVEMENT PROCESS
   Actual: 1   2   3   4
   Desired: 1   2   3   4
7. PERSONNEL QUALITY DESIRED
   Actual: 1   2   3   4
   Desired: 1   2   3   4
8. IMPORTANCE OF INCENTIVES
   Actual: 1   2   3   4
   Desired: 1   2   3   4
9. IMPORTANCE OF EVALUATION
   Actual: 1   2   3   4
   Desired: 1   2   3   4

and your colleagues perceive as the actual situation and what you want as the desired. You then can use a problem-solving process to make the changes indicated.

USING SCHOOL-BASED MANAGEMENT

School-based management (sometimes called site-based management) can be the process used to apply transformational concepts—or it can simply be a process of instituting the old style, but at the school level instead of the district level. The concern, therefore, is for *quality* school-based management. To help you achieve this goal, this section clarifies the concept and presents a rationale for it, describes how school-based models work, reviews the research on their effectiveness, and suggests some steps you and your colleagues can use in using school-based models.

The Concept and Its Rationale

First, let's be sure about the term. One of the best definitions is offered by Lindelow and Heynderickx (1989):

School-based management is a system of administration in which the school is the primary unit of educational decision-making. (p. 109)

Why is school-based management crucial in school-improvement efforts? First, the school is the main locus of change. As the literature on school effectiveness suggests, most long-term improvement comes about by making schools better; it is much more difficult to transform school systems. Now, if the school is the locus of change, then it makes sense to place most of the decision-making at the school level. Doing so is more likely to make improvement efforts successful because those involved in making schools better are given an active role in deciding how to do so. Also, locating most of the decision-making at the school level is more likely to improve the quality of those decisions because school-based educators have a better understanding of the special context of that school. Finally, school-based decision-making is more likely to increase the morale of teachers because they prefer organizations in which they have an active voice.

How School-Based Management Works

As noted by Clune and White (1988), there are so many different forms of school-based management that it is difficult to generalize. The process usually begins with the initiative from an activist superintendent, who persuades the school board to adopt policies facilitating school-based management. These policies and their accompanying procedures are usually formulated into a contract or "charter." Each school then sets up its own school-based management advisory council, composed of the school principal, along with representatives of the following constituencies: teachers, parents, and (at the high school) students. The advisory council is provided with the necessary training.

The council then executes its advisory functions in four major areas. First, it advises the principal and team leaders in selecting teachers who wish to join the faculty, to ensure that they are receiving teachers who share the school's values. Second, it institutes a process of school-based curriculum development, taking steps to ensure that the curricula produced achieve district goals. It advises about budgeting priorities, recommending fiscal decisions that reflect school priorities. Finally, it reviews and recommends modifications of the school's improvement plans and receives periodic reports on progress and problems.

In all these matters, the council actively involves all the teachers and as many parents as it can. If any of its recommendations seem to be at odds with federal or state regulations, board policies, or the union contract, the council requests waivers. (Both the National Education Association and the American Federation of Teachers have approved bargaining procedures that will permit the temporary suspension of contract provisions during school-improvement efforts.) The amount of power wielded by the council seems to vary considerably. In most schools, it has only an advisory role; however, in some schools they have decision-making authority.

In all operations, the school board, the superintendent, and the council emphasize four process components: *involvement,* securing the active participation of an enlarged community—including noncertified personnel; *empowerment,* conferring increased authority on the school team and advancing its autonomy; *restructuring,* focusing energies on comprehensive improvement plans; and *accountability,* holding itself and others accountable for results. (See Mojkowski and Fleming 1988, for a discussion of these components.)

One of the exemplary approaches to school-based management is the NEA Mastery in Learning Project, a network of schools that use school-based management approaches to school improvement. In each of the schools, teachers examine and share information, formulate research questions, establish task forces, and test strategies.

The Research on School-Based Management

Because there is a relatively thin research base on school-based management, the research findings that follow should be seen as somewhat tentative. (The findings are drawn primarily from three excellent reviews: White 1989; David 1989; and Malen, Ogawa, and Kranz.)

First, there is no consistent evidence that school-based management itself increases student achievement. As White points out, it is difficult, if not impossible, to sort out the effects of school-based management from other local improvement initiatives. Malen and her colleagues are even more negative about this issue. They conclude that "student achievement does not appear to be either helped or hindered" (p. 59).

Second, the evidence of its effects on teacher morale are somewhat mixed. David concludes from her review that, when given real authority, teachers report increased satisfaction, "even exuberance" (p. 51). Malen and colleagues are more skeptical. Their findings suggest that any improvement in morale is fleeting. The initial enthusiasm turns to frustration and disappointment as teachers encounter problems with time, with the complexity of the problems they face, and with the conflict between their leadership and teaching responsibilities.

Finally, the research is again mixed on the effects on the decision-making process. David reports that school-based management teams have made important decisions concerning staffing, personnel, curriculum, and the daily schedule. Malen and colleagues conclude that school-based management teams rarely exert substantial influence on school-policy decisions.

In addition to this generally inconclusive evidence, researchers have noted the following drawbacks and problems associated with school-based management efforts:

- In some cases, the district had ceded too much of its authority, leading to a lack of coordination and articulation throughout the district. Most experts in organizational theory seem to recommend a balanced authority structure that captures the advantages of both centralization and decentralization.

- School-based management demands major time commitments from teachers, who already feel overloaded. Most teachers believe that their primary responsibility is instruction. They view participation in school-based management as a luxury that they may not be able to afford.

- School-based management often results in a power struggle among administrators, teachers, parents, and students. Rather than cooperating, these individuals compete to gain greater authority.

- Most school-based management programs suffer from a scarcity of resources. Power over the budget may be

173

meaningless when there are very few discretionary funds available.

- The seeming transfer of power may be only superficial and trivial. In their study of the Salt Lake City (Utah) school-based management program, Malen and Ogawa (1988) concluded that teachers and parents did not wield significant influence on major issues that came to the advisory council meetings. They noted several obstacles to real power-sharing: the councils were highly homogeneous in membership, with minorities obviously excluded; principals saw the councils only as "forums for input," not as real decision-making bodies; principals continued to retain power, with teachers and parents seemingly reluctant to challenge the administrators; all seemed to have an implicit understanding that certain major issues were outside the purview of the council; and all operated with a norm of civility that made meaningful conflict rather rare.

Developing Your Own School-Based Program

This somewhat discouraging view of school-based management should not lead you to ignore its potential. You and your colleagues can learn from those schools that have struggled to find effective solutions to the problems described earlier. Those school-based field reports would suggest that you and your colleagues, along with the principal, take the following steps in developing and implementing your own model:

1. *Negotiate carefully the initial agreement on the specific issues involved in the school-based model.* Give special attention to the balance between centralization and decentralization. Figure 10-3 suggests how I see that balance. It includes the major aspects examined in this book, along with a few others (such as budgeting). For each aspect, both the role of the district and the school are noted. I encourage you to use them as guidelines for your own analyses.

174

Figure 10-3
DISTRICT AND SCHOOL AUTHORITY

ASPECT/LOCUS	SCHOOL DISTRICT	SCHOOL
CURRICULUM	Identifies goals, objectives, and priorities	Develops units Determines sequence Suggests activities
STAFF DEVELOPMENT	Trains leaders Sets policies Provides resources	Operates school-based programs
STUDENT MOTIVATION PROGRAMS	Sets policy guidelines Provides resources	Develops, implements, and evaluates programs
HOME/SCHOOL RELATIONSHIPS	Sets policy guidelines Provides resources	Develops, implements, and evaluates programs
SCHOOL SCHEDULES	Specifies parameters Sets policy guidelines	Develops, implements, and evaluates its own schedule
ASSESSMENT PROGRAM	Establishes policies for evaluation of personnel Develops district program to evaluate student achievement	Implements policies Develops school-based program to evaluate student learning Uses evaluation data for school improvement *(continued)*

ASPECT/LOCUS	SCHOOL DISTRICT	SCHOOL
BUDGET	Establishes guidelines Allocates budget to school on basis of enrollment	Makes budget allocations based on needs and priorities
PERSONNEL	Establishes policy and procedures guidelines Allocates overall staffing resources	Selects and assigns staff
INSTRUCTIONAL MATERIALS	Sets guidelines Establishes reviews procedures Makes allotments	Evaluates and selects instructional materials
INSTRUCTIONAL MODEL	Supports effective instruction	Determines models to be used

Also, spell out as precisely as you can what methods of accountability you will use. Consider each area, specify your long-range goal, and indicate how your performance will be evaluated.

2. *Determine the functions the school-based management advisory council will serve.* You have three choices here: the council can serve only as an advisory group; it can serve as a decision-making group; or it can advise about some issues and decide about others. My own recommendation is that the council have only an advisory function, but this matter needs to be examined and resolved at the local level. As will be explained more fully below, I believe that the major decisions about program and personnel should be made by the school's leadership council, composed only of the members of the professional staff.

   With the council's function clearly established, the next step is to choose the members, being sure to get a representative group that includes all constituencies.

3. *Establish goals for the first year.* The research studies that have examined effective school-based programs conclude that such programs moved at a deliberate pace, rather than trying to do too much at once. A long-term plan should be developed, so that there is an overall design; but the first year of operation should focus on clearly attainable goals. Some researchers note that it will take as long as five or six years to establish a comprehensive school-based program.

4. *Provide the training needed.* All those actively involved in the project should be provided with the training they need to function effectively. This is especially important for the advisory council because it brings together several individuals who have not previously worked with each other. Several of those who have been involved with school-based programs stress the critical need for providing training in such areas as group problem-solving, conflict resolution, planning, and communicating (Harrison, Killion, and Mitchell 1989).

5. *Implement a systematic and incremental planning process.* Chapter 11 in this book explains a planning process that you and your colleagues can use in planning and implementing your school-based model. Be sure to provide the planners with the resources they need to accomplish their job. As pointed out by Malen, Ogawa, and Kranz (1990), many school-based teams do not plan well because they lack the time, the technical assistance, or the logistical support to develop and implement effective plans.

6. *Focus on quality and substance.* In making substantive changes, keep in mind Deming's injunction to build in quality throughout the entire process. Encourage the planners to make high quality substantive changes, rather than fussing with trivialities.

7. *Monitor and adjust.* One key feature of that planning model is to monitor programs periodically and make adjustments, building in quality as you progress.

TEAM LEADERSHIP

Whether or not you have or plan to have school-based management, you should still consider establishing a strong and viable system of team leadership. Team leadership does not minimize the role of the principal. It simply capitalizes on the strengths of the entire faculty.

Team Leadership: A Rationale and Overview

At the outset, it would be useful to examine some broad issues as they relate to teacher involvement in leadership and decision-making before turning to structural considerations.

There are two major reasons for involving teachers in leadership roles. The first involves the impact on teachers of what has been termed *decision-deprivation*, a feeling that one would like to have more influence on decision-making. In a review of research on this issue during a 20-year period, Conley (1991) concludes that when teachers feel deprived of decision-making opportunities, they report more dissatisfaction, more stress, and less loyalty to principals.

The second reason involves the impact on the school organization. As Shedd and Bacharach (1991) note, teacher involvement is likely to result in better decisions. Because teachers participate daily in the critical action in the classroom, they have better data about those central issues of student motivation, student discipline, and student learning. The view of one teacher about school life is restricted and narrow; but, the views of all teachers are broad and multi-dimensional. Conley also notes that teacher participation in decision making also leads to increased collegiality, one of the key norms of effective schools. Involvement also enhances effectiveness, efficiency, and productivity by improving the organization's ability to respond quickly to problems (Shedd and Bacharach 1991).

How extensively are teachers involved in decision making? A recent report indicates that there has been little progress in the last few years and that teachers are still frozen out of the decision-making process in several vital areas (Carnegie Foundation for the Advancement of Teaching 1990). The report notes these examples of decision-deprivation (the figures indicate the percentage of teachers who feel they are involved either "slightly" or "not at all"): setting student promotion policies, 71 percent; budget, 80 percent; selection of new teachers, 90 percent; evaluating teacher performance, 93 percent. Conley observes that teachers feel most deprived in those areas that fall on the boundary between classroom and the school organization: student rights, reporting procedures, and grading policies.

Structures for Involvement

Perhaps the best way to achieve more meaningful and extensive involvement of teachers in decision making and leadership is through a comprehensive restructuring of the school as an organization. The restructuring recommended here involves the use of leadership and instructional teams. This section will present some principles to guide such restructuring and present an overview of the restructured organization. It will then examine in closer detail the major components.

Principles of Team Organization

What principles should guide you and your colleagues in organizing teams? The following principles and their corollaries are drawn from the literature on organizational change and teaming as well as from this author's experience in working with teams.

- *Instruction is central.* Any team organization should support the instructional ends of schooling. It follows, therefore, that instructional teams should reflect the basic emphasis of the instructional program. If grade-level integration is foremost, then the instructional teams should have a grade-level structure; if the subject is primary, then the teams should have a subject focus.

- *Leadership is collegial.* While the principal needs to play an active role, schools are more effective when leadership is distributed among the instructional teams. Therefore, a leadership council composed of instructional team leaders can provide direction for the school.

- *Coordination is necessary.* Coordination is needed between the leadership council and the instructional teams. It is also needed between teachers at the same grade level. Finally, it is needed within a subject, across grade levels.

- *Flexibility matters.* Specific school-wide problems are best attacked and solved by *ad hoc* groups that are organized to focus on a particular issue and are then dissolved when their mission has been accomplished.

- *Advice is needed from a variety of viewpoints.* Students and parents need to be heard. Their input can make the problem-solving process more effective.

- *Teachers and administrators are very busy people.* Therefore, the number of committees should be kept to an absolute minimum.

Overview of the Restructured Organization

How can you operationalize those principles and their corollaries? Obviously, the answer is best determined locally because the answers are very much affected by such contextual factors as size of faculty, maturity of the staff, and the competence of the principal. The following description represents my attempt to make sense of the literature and my own experience in working with teams.

The core group is the instructional team, groups of teachers who are responsible for the instruction of a large number of students. The instructional team may be organized by grade level, as in the elementary school, or by subjects, as in the high school. Each instructional team is led by a team leader, who also serves as a member of the leadership council. The leadership council is the decision-making body that includes the principal, the assistant principal, and the team leaders. The leadership council is advised by the school-based management advisory council.

Two other groups also function. In addition to having a primary assignment to the instructional team, each teacher also serves on a coordination team. The purpose of the coordination team is to complement the instructional team by exercising a coordinating function. If the instructional team is organized by grade level, then the coordinating team is organized by subject. Thus, Harold Jones, a fifth grade teacher who is strong in mathematics, would have a primary responsibility to the fifth grade instructional team but would also chair the mathematics coordinating team. If the instructional team is organized by subjects, then the coordinating team is structured on a grade-level basis. Thus, Eleanor Miskel, a chemistry teacher, has a primary responsibility to the high school science team. But, she also serves on the eleventh grade coordinating team.

Finally, the leadership council appoints and monitors the work of several task forces, *ad hoc* groups that are given the responsibility of solving problems related to a substantive issue. Thus, your school might have a task force on student motivation and a task force on school climate.

With that big picture clarified, let's turn our attention now to a more detailed view of how these groups might operate. The following discussion examines these groups: instructional teams, the leadership council, the coordination teams, and the task forces. (The advisory council was discussed in the above session.)

A Closer Look at Instructional Teams

As mentioned earlier, the instructional team is central. The entire faculty is organized into teaching teams that are responsible for the instructional program of a large number of students. Here are some patterns of organization that have been used successfully:

The Grade Level Team

In this pattern, used chiefly in elementary school, all teachers who teach at a particular grade level are assigned to a grade-level team. Specialists (such as in the fields of art and music), who teach many grades, are assigned to one of the grade-level teams.

The Departmental Team

In this pattern, used predominantly at the high school level, all teachers who teach in a given field of study (such as science or mathematics) are assigned to a subject-focused team. Teachers in single-person departments (such as home economics and art) are grouped into a department that is then given a general term (such as "fine and practical arts").

The House Team

Larger schools are divided into smaller "houses" or "schools-within-schools." Each house is staffed with a team of teachers that represents all the subjects taught and all the grade levels included. The same approach can be used in a nongraded elementary school, without specific concern for grade-level specialization.

Obviously, there is no single best approach. Just keep two recommendations in mind. First, each teacher should have only *one* primary team assignment, not two or three. Second, structure should follow program. If you want interdisciplinary curricula, use interdisciplinary teams; if you want subject-focused teaching, use departmental teams.

Each team should choose its own leader, who should be required to meet specified criteria. The leader should have demonstrated expertise in teaching, played an active and constructive role in school improvement, and displayed the ability to work effectively with others. Team leaders should be appointed for a specified term, such as three or four years.

Team leaders can exercise six critical functions, according to Devaney (1987). They can: (1) continue to teach and improve their own teaching, (2) organize and lead well-informed peer reviews of school practice, (3) participate productively in school-level decision making, (4) organize and lead inservice education, (5) advise and assist individual teachers, and (6) participate in the performance evaluation of teachers.

You and your colleagues should decide how many of these functions your team leaders should perform. The team is centrally responsible for the instruction of a large group of students. Team members make decisions about all the essential areas involving the instruction of those students, in each case operating within school guidelines. Areas include: the use of time, student grouping, student discipline, and teacher assignments.

In addition to these areas of instructional decision-making, teams are actively involved in several other areas of school life. Figure 10-4 analyzes the major functions that teams can perform, along with some examples for each. Those functions are arranged in order of increasing complexity. Again, working within guidelines established at the school level, each team would decide which of these eight functions it wishes to perform as a team.

It is hoped that all teams as they mature can undertake all eight functions. To do so effectively, of course, they will need ample time and effective training. Time especially is critical. How much time they require for team meetings would obviously depend on the extent of their team work. Very active teams would probably need one period each day for regular planning and one double period each week for special team activities.

Leadership Council

The leadership council is the key decision-making group about matters that go beyond the team instructional areas. It is composed of the school administrators, the leaders of the instructional teams, and a representative of those providing support services (guidance, health, and library). Its central responsibility lies with school improvement and with the central matters of school governance, not with the details of school operation.

The cycle of school improvement for which it is responsible includes the periodic assessments recommended in Chapter 8. In addition, it plans and implements an end-of-year needs assessment, using available data to identify school-improvement targets. All those assessment results are built into a comprehensive school-improvement plan that becomes the basis for budgeting for the coming school year.

When the new school year begins, the leadership council implements the improvement plan for that year. Each major program initiative is under the direction of the *ad hoc* task force

Figure 10-4
FUNCTIONS OF THE INSTRUCTIONAL TEAM

FUNCTIONS	EXAMPLES
1. PLAN	Exchange lesson plans Develop common plans Critique plans
2. SCHEDULE	Allocate time Group students
3. DIAGNOSE STUDENT PROBLEMS	Identify and diagnose problems of learning, motivation, and discipline Make referrals
4. TEACH	Exchange classes Present lessons together Assist in large group sessions Lead small group seminars
5. ASSESS LEARNING	Develop, administer, and evaluate alternative forms of assessment
6. DEVELOP CURRICULA AND INSTRUCTIONAL MATERIALS	Develop integrated units Develop enrichment and remediation materials
7. IDENTIFY ORGANIZATIONAL PROBLEMS	Monitor learning and organizational climate Identify developing problems
8. PROVIDE FOR PROFESSIONAL DEVELOPMENT	Induct new teachers Use peer coaching Conduct action research Conduct professional dialogues

(explained more fully later). During the new school year, the council actively monitors the progress of the plan, relying on data supplied by the instructional teams and the coordinating teams. If a major problem develops, it appoints a new task force to examine and analyze the problem and propose a solution.

In addition to school-improvement planning, the leadership council develops (with input from the instructional teams) broad guidelines and policies in the following areas: teacher scheduling, student rights, school security, parent-teacher relationships, teacher evaluation, and budgeting. All those guidelines and policies are cycled back to the instructional teams for analysis and discussion before being adopted by the entire faculty.

To summarize, the leadership council accomplishes several major functions. It evaluates the present program, uses evaluation data to develop a school-improvement plan, provides leadership in the implementation of the plan, monitors progress, appoints problem-solving task forces as needed, and develops broad guidelines and policies on school-wide issues.

How frequently the council meets depends upon the level of activity at a given point in time. Typically, one two-hour session every two weeks would be sufficient to provide time for problem analysis and solution. Additional time would be needed when considering major changes in policy areas.

The Coordinating Teams

The coordinating teams play a less active role. Typically, they would meet only once a month, or as needed. Keep in mind that their central purpose is to complement the instructional teams.

Let's examine more closely how they perform their coordinating function in two modes—as an adjunct to grade-level teams and as an adjunct to departmental teams.

Adjunct to Grade-Level Teams

The grade-level teams are essentially learner-centered, using the perspective of a single grade or age group. What they miss is the subject focus, with a multi-grade perspective. For this reason, four coordinating teams are needed, one for each of the major subjects: reading and English language arts, social studies, mathematics, and science. Each teacher chooses the coordinating team he or she wishes to be a part of. The coordinating team is headed by a classroom teacher with special competence in that subject area.

Once a month, the coordinating teams meet. Teachers raise instructional problems and share ideas and materials. They look most closely at coordination from grade to grade. They examine the curriculum closely. They identify problems of coordination that may need the attention of the leadership council.

Adjunct to Departmental Teams

At the high school level, the coordinating teams focus on inter-subject coordination at a given grade level. Here, they are organized by grade; thus, at the high school, there would be four teams, one for each high school grade. Consider, for example, how the Tenth Grade Coordinating Team might operate. Members would examine the entire program of studies for tenth grade, asking the following questions: Is there a good balance between required subjects and electives? Are all subjects allocated time in a way that reflects their curricular priority? Team members would also examine issues of coordination by asking questions such as: Should some of the math content be shifted so that it provides greater support to the science curriculum? Should the English curriculum be modified so that it relates more closely to the social studies curriculum?

The high school coordinating teams are also the best place for integrated units to be developed.

Task Forces

The task forces are problem-solving groups, composed of teachers and administrators with special competence and interest in the problem addressed. To see how they might operate, consider this situation. By analyzing data from the instructional teams, the leadership council has determined that student motivation is a problem. The council appoints a Student Motivation Task Force, led by a teacher with special knowledge of the research on motivation.

Under that teacher's leadership, the task force uses the following problem-solving process. They:

1. *Analyze the "mess."* The mess refers to a general sense of some deficiency. Rather than prematurely identifying the problem, the task force undertakes a systematic analysis to understand the mess. It would use surveys, observations, interviews, and analysis of assessment data to determine the following: Which students seem especially unmotivated? Are there subjects or classes where the motivation seems especially low? How do students perceive the mess? How do parents perceive it?

2. *Define the problem.* Based upon that analysis, task-force members then clearly and sharply define the problem. They pose it in this fashion: How might we help minority students increase their level of motivation in academic subjects?

3. *Build the knowledge base.* Before they generate solutions, task-force members develop their knowledge base. They review the research. They investigate exemplary programs. They discern and distill their own knowledge. This gathering and distillation of knowledge leads to the publication and dissemination of a report to the entire faculty: "What we know about minority student motivation to learn."

4. *Generate possible solutions.* Now the task force uses its new knowledge and feedback from the faculty to generate creative solutions. At this stage, all criticism and negativism is ruled out.

5. *Critique possible solutions.* Now the task force adopts a critical stance by asking the following: Which solutions are most

likely to work? What resources will they require? How likely are they to be accepted?

6. *Develop a solution package.* As a result of their critique, task-force members develop a solution package—a set of specific responses to the problem that work together and reinforce each other. For example, the solution package for the student motivation problem might include the following: modify the curriculum, work with parents, and modify the extra-curricular program.

That solution package is then presented to the leadership council for its review, modification, and adoption.

FOR FURTHER READING

Bailey , W.J. 1991. *School-site management applied.* Lancaster, Penn.: Technomic. Gives very useful suggestions for developing school-based management programs.

Erb, T.O. and Doda, N.M. 1989. *Team organization: Promise, practices, and possibilities.* Washington, D.C.: National Education Association. Provides very helpful information how teams can work together in solving specific problems.

Johnson, D.W. and Johnson, R.T. 1989. *Leading the cooperative school.* Edina, Minn.: Interaction Book. Presents a comprehensive analysis of the teaching and learning processes and the leadership structure in a truly cooperative school.

REFERENCES

Blankenstein, A.M. 1992. Lessons from enlightened corporations. *Educational Leadership* , 49(6): 71–5.

Brandt, R. 1992. On rethinking leadership: A conversation with Tom Sergiovanni. *Educational Leadership,* 49(5): 46–9.

Burns, J.M. 1978. *Leadership.* New York: Harper and Row.

Carnegie Foundation for the Advancement of Teaching. 1990. *The condition of teaching: A state-by-state analysis,* 1990. New York: Carnegie Foundation for the Advancement of Teaching.

Clune, W.H. and White, P.A. 1988. *School-based management: Institutional variation, implementation, and issues for further research.* New Brunswick, N.J.: Center for Policy Research in Education, Rutgers University.

Conley, S. 1991. Review of research on teacher participation in school decision making. In *Review of research in education,* vol. 17, ed. G. Grant, 225–68. Washington, D.C.: American Educational Research Association.

David, J.L. 1989. Synthesis of research on school-based management. *Educational Leadership,* 46(9): 45–53.

Deming, W.E. 1988. *Out of the crisis.* Cambridge, Mass.: Massachusetts Institute of Technology.

Devaney, K. 1987. *The lead teacher: Ways to begin.* New York: Carnegie Forum on Education and the Economy.

Harrison, C.R.; Killion, J.P.; and Mitchell, J.E. 1989. Site-based management: The realities of implementation. *Educational Leadership,* 46(9): 55–8.

Leithwood, K.A. 1992. The move toward transformational leadership. *Educational leadership,* 49(5): 8–12.

Lindelow, J. and Heynderickx, J. 1989. School-based management. In *School leadership: Handbook for excellence,* eds. S.C. Smith and P.K. Piele, 109–34. Eugene, Ore.: ERIC Clearinghouse on Educational Management, University of Oregon.

Malen, B. and Ogawa, R.T. 1988. Professional-patron influence on site-based governance councils: A confounding case study. *Educational Evaluation and Policy Analysis,* vol. 10, 251–70.

Malen, B.; Ogawa, R.T.; and Kranz, J. 1990. Site-based management: Unfulfilled promises. *School Administrator*, 47(2): 30–2; 53–9.

Mojkowski, C. and Fleming, D. 1988. *School-site management: Concepts and approaches*. Andover, Mass.: Regional Laboratory for Educational Improvement of the Northeast and Islands.

Sergiovanni, T.J. 1992. Why we should seek substitutes for leadership. *Educational Leadership*, 49(5): 41–5.

Shedd, J.B. and Bacharach, S.B. 1991. *Tangled hierarchies: Teachers as professionals and the management of schools*. San Francisco: Jossey Bass.

White, P.A. 1989. An overview of school-based management: What does the research say? *NASSP Bulletin*, 76(527): 1–8.

Chapter 11

SYSTEMATIC AND INCREMENTAL PLANNING

All of the changes recommended in this book require systematic planning. Increasingly, researchers in the change process are recommending that such changes be implemented incrementally as well as in a dynamic and an interactive manner. This chapter draws upon this growing body of research to suggest how you and your colleagues can bring about change.

UNDERSTANDING THE CHANGE PROCESS

For years, educators have followed a rational and linear change model that seemed to produce innovations that did not last. Current researchers who have examined the nature of successful and unsuccessful change are now advocating a very different model. Perhaps the best summary of that new model is presented in the work of Louis and Miles (1990), the primary source for the following generalizations on successful change.

- *Successful change is vision-driven.* The vision gives larger meaning to the change efforts by placing school changes in the context of the larger society. In this sense, the vision is more important than goals, which tend to focus solely on internal changes.

- *Successful change is guided by judgment, not rules.* Educational change is a complex process that escapes the confines of rules and regulations. It is better guided by the professional judgment of administrators and teachers.

- *Successful change is accountability-based.* Groups are held accountable for performance, not for procedures. A group charged with a specific task is expected to produce results, not excuses.

- *Successful change is team-based and team-driven.* Rather than using an outmoded hierarchical approach to leadership, effective schools use cooperative teams to produce results. The principal still plays a very critical role, but the role is one of motivating, informing, coordinating, and monitoring.

- *Successful change is network-based and semi-autonomous.* The school is seen as part of an interconnected web of relationships, not as an isolated part of a bureaucratic machine. The school is connected to its community, to its classrooms, to its district, and to its state. It has both autonomy and connectedness.

- *Successful change requires people who are multi-specialized.* Similar to industry's concern for worker flexibility, schools need administrators and teachers who can perform a variety of roles. The professional teacher, for example, must be a curriculum developer, a staff developer, a problem-solver, and a counselor as well as an effective instructor.

- *Successful change is involved with the whole person.* Increasingly, schools see a need to accept responsibility for coordinating and providing a wide variety of educational and social services.

It is also important to realize that successful change varies in impact. According to Cuban (1988), there are two levels of change. *First-order changes* are relatively superficial changes that simply refine the present way schools operate, teachers teach, and children learn. An example would be a project to align the existing curriculum so that the written, the taught, the tested, and the supported curriculum are all congruent. *Second-order changes,* on the other hand, are more radical and comprehensive, attempting to alter the foundations of education. An example is the development of a totally integrated curriculum that ignores all subject matter distinctions.

Cuban uses these constructs to explain why so-called "reform" has failed under the old model of change: under the old linear way, first-order changes succeeded, but made little difference; second-order changes were undermined by teachers

194

and administrators who saw no gain and much loss in the ambitious plans of a handful of reformers who seemed blissfully unaware of the realities of schools and classrooms.

The new model is a more challenging one. It requires the active involvement of many reflective, realistic professionals, but it is more likely to produce long-lasting change.

Stages of the Change Process

Change can perhaps best be understood as occurring in several interactive stages. *Preliminary planning* involves the general tasks of developing a comprehensive vision of long-term change and building a flexible schedule for specific innovations. *Initiation* follows preliminary planning. It is the process that leads up to and includes the decision to adopt a specific change. *Implementation,* usually the first two or three years of use (Fullan 1991), involves the first attempts to put the innovation into practice. *Continuation* is the stage in which the innovation becomes fully incorporated into the system. Some call this stage "institutionalization," emphasizing the fact that the change becomes a deep-seated part of the innovation or is institution-alized. All together, these stages would require from five to 10 years for complex restructuring programs, Fullan notes.

The discussion in the latter part of this chapter, explaining how to bring about a change, focuses on the first three stages because they seem most critical.

Guidelines for the Change Process

Many educators believe these myths about the change process:

- Wide-spread participation and involvement are crucial at the outset.
- The bigger the change, the better.
- Always be democratic, using bottom-up processes.
- Change teachers' attitudes before you implement a change.

- A strong leader with a clear vision of the change can be successful in imposing innovations.
- Develop and implement complex planning processes during the implementation stage.

The available research suggests that these beliefs are not valid. Consider, instead, the "research-based maxims" presented in Figure 11-1 (Fullan 1991 and Louis and Miles 1990).

MAKING PRELIMINARY PLANNING MORE EFFECTIVE

Let's assume that you and your colleagues in cooperation with your principal have decided to undertake comprehensive school reform by using several of the programmatic changes discussed in this book. First, you will need to establish a small team of administrators and teachers to provide leadership in the preliminary planning process. (You can use the leadership council explained in the previous chapter, an existing school improvement team, or a new group.) That group should provide leadership in helping the faculty accomplish the tasks that follow.

1. *Begin with a preliminary assessment of needs.* Take a month to gather and analyze available data to determine potential strengths and weaknesses. Check such data sources as student achievement, student attendance, student disciplinary referrals, student-health problems, curriculum guides, classroom observations, school-climate surveys, and surveys of teacher perceptions.

2. *Build the knowledge base.* By reviewing the chapters in this book and other current and reliable sources, determine what programs and approaches seem to have worked with students like yours.

3. *Develop your own comprehensive long-term school improvement model.* Rather than jumping on some current bandwagon that

196

Figure 11-1

THE ELEVEN MAXIMS OF THE CHANGE PROCESS

1. Large-scale participation at the initiation stage may be counter-productive.
2. The size of the change matters. The change should be large enough to require sustained effort, but not so massive that it overwhelms participants.
3. Leaders should be flexible and multiple in the approach to change, blending top-down and bottom-up processes. They should have a plan, but be ready to learn by doing.
4. For change to be successful, administrators need both to apply pressure and provide support.
5. Changes in attitude often follow changes in behavior. Most people do not discover new meanings until they have tried something new.
6. Leadership that is strongly committed to a particular type of change is negatively related to the ability to adopt it. In other words, the leader who is positive that he or she knows exactly how things should be changed ignores the perceptions and ideas of others and thus runs the risk of failure.
7. While planning is important, complicated implementation plans can become a burden and a source of confusion.
8. Some problems are unsolvable. They are better left alone.
9. Use "positive politics"—focus on a few important priorities by implementing them well while keeping other priorities in perspective.
10. Act and then plan. Adopt an action orientation and solve important problems. Effective action often stimulates interest in planning.
11. The most important priorities should be developing people and changing the culture of the organization. Placing those goals first develops the school's capacity for making effective change.

(Sources: Fullan 1991, Louis and Miles 1990.)

will rush by and then disappear, build your own home-grown model that reflects your needs and your vision of where you want to go. Figure 11-2 shows how your model might look at this stage.

Note that the set of statements about the model is framed as a general set of commitments. It is clearly focused, but not overly specific.

The statements are what Louis and Miles (1990) call *themes*. As they use the term, themes are interim change goals that help to organize and direct energy. They note that often the themes develop into a vision, as they become linked, achieve success, and are owned by participants. The statement of commitments or themes should be produced initially by the leadership team, reviewed by the entire faculty and representative parents in open discussions, and modified accordingly.

4. *Develop a tentative long-term calendar that indicates, year by year, how you hope to operationalize those themes.* You need to choose one theme or interim improvement-goal that you will emphasize initially. Choose an improvement goal that is likely to make an impact and is not too difficult to achieve. You want to make a difference, but you also want to experience initial success. Then you want to phase in the other components so that you link the themes and achieve your vision, without overtaxing the system.

Several elements in the sample planning schedule shown in Figure 11-3 deserve special attention here. First, the developers distinguished between programmatic changes—specific programs that could be initiated, implemented, and continued—and ongoing activities that would be fostered throughout the project. For example, staff development is not a programmatic change that you initiate once and then implement. It is an ongoing process that provides support at every stage.

198

Figure 11-2

LINCOLN ELEMENTARY SCHOOL'S
MODEL OF SCHOOL IMPROVEMENT

We're on the road to excellence. During the next five years we will work with the school board, the district office, and the community to achieve excellence through the following initiatives:

1. *We will change the school culture.* We will emphasize these positive values: success for everyone; the school is a learning community; collaboration and cooperation are essential, and improvement should be continuous.
2. *We will put our trust in our professionals.* We will provide high quality staff-development programs for administrators and teachers.
3. *We will work with parents.* We will consider them to be equal partners in the shared enterprise of educating our children and youth.
4. *We will provide excellent teaching.* We will use technology and cooperative learning effectively, and we will actively involve all students in the learning process.
5. *We will increase student motivation to learn.* We will plan, implement, and evaluate special programs to increase this motivation.
6. *We will offer a dynamic, future-oriented curriculum.* We will produce a curriculum that responds to multicultural diversity, teaches problem-solving, and emphasizes information processing.

Second, the planners allowed one year for initiation of each programmatic change and two years for implementation. In doing so, they were careful not to overload the system.

Note also that they decided to begin with a project to improve student motivation. While they realized that it would be a complex task, they believed that the teachers were concerned about motivation, and they knew that more motivated students would achieve greater learning. In identifying the initial project, Fullan (1991) suggests that you choose one of high quality and relevance. High quality innovations are those that will make an impact on learning. Those with relevance are judged by teachers to be responsive to the needs they have identified.

Finally, the schedule exemplifies the recommendations of experts that planners should "think big and begin small." The developers had a general sense of where they were headed. They began with one focused project that would take them closer to that generalized goal.

Figure 11-3

LONG-TERM PLANNING CALENDAR

Schedule for Programmatic Improvements:

	Year 1	Year 2	Year 3	Year 4	Year 5
Parents		Initiate	Implement	Implement	Continue
Teaching				Initiate	Implement
Student motiva-tion	Initiate	Implement	Implement	Continue	Continue
Curricu-lum			Initiate	Implement	Implement

MAKING THE INITIATION STAGE MORE PRODUCTIVE

Now we are ready to examine the change process as it involves one specific programmatic innovation, moving through the stages of initiation and implementation. In discussing both stages, the analysis will use a new student-motivation program for the sake of illustration.

Remember that in the initiation stage you are primarily concerned with taking the initial steps needed to get the program off to a sound start. Typically, the initiation stage lasts one year, although time is obviously affected by the complexity of the change and the resources available. The following steps are those you should take in making the initiation stage more productive.

- *Step One.* First, appoint a task force of administrators and teachers that will be responsible for managing this specific project. Administrators must be involved at the outset; their active participation sends an strong message to the teachers that the project is worthy of their support.

- *Step Two.* Next, the task force should institute an evolutionary planning process. That evolutionary planning process has three key features. It first involves setting some broad goals that are vague enough to provide flexibility as the program develops. Specific and narrow goals can constrain flexibility. Here is the goal that the planners of the motivation project posed for the school: *Enable our students to increase their motivation to learn.*

  Second, it is designed so that it moves control from administrators to teachers. While administrative support is crucial, the intent is to turn over the innovation to the teachers so that they feel greater power and accountability.

  Third, the evolutionary planning process is flexible. Data are gathered on a continuing basis to assess progress and identify problems. Emerging problems are solved before they become too critical. As new needs develop, new initiatives are undertaken.

- *Step Three.* Part of that evolutionary planning process is the development of a flexible calendar. The calendar is developed by identifying the major components of the program, determining which steps are needed to operationalize each component, and indicating a reasonable target date for each step. An example is shown in Figure 11-4; the example shows the first six months of an 11-month initiation cycle. Note that the planning calendar includes an *administration* strand, in which the planners have recorded all the major administrative tasks that must be accomplished, and an *evaluation* strand, in which the formative assessment processes have been noted. In addition to those two elements, the plans have also included as strands all the major components of their program.

- *Step Four.* The next step is to build support at the district level. Even though the change is school-based, it would still be essential for the superintendent and the central office staff to be very supportive. The research indicates that strong administrative pressure is essential for success. That top-down pressure accompanied by bottom-up development and im-plementation sustains effective change.

- *Step Five.* With that district support established, you now need to secure the resources you will need. Louis and Miles suggest that you find funds to pay a new staff member to direct the program. If funds cannot be found to support a full-time person, then work toward getting release time for one of the teachers. Also be sure that planners provide time for teachers to develop the program, funds to travel to exemplary programs, and professional materials for the staff development program.

- *Step Six.* Next, keep teachers fully informed and involved at the outset and provide them with the initial training they will need to implement the program effectively. Keep in mind that their initial concerns will focus on understanding the new program and becoming clear about its immediate impact upon them. At this point program clarity is vital. The research on change indicates that many innovations fail because the planners and initiators have not really been clear about what they are trying to do (Louis and Miles 1990).

- *Step Seven.* Also during the initiation stage you may wish to focus on some immediate task you can accomplish, rather than spending all the time on planning. Increasingly, researchers are suggesting an "act-plan" strategy in which you solve some pressing problem to demonstrate your capacity to act. For example, the teachers in West Craven High School (Craven

Figure 11-4
DETAILED PLANNING: INITIATION

	Sept.	Oct.	Nov.	Dec.	Jan.	Feb.
Administration	Gather district support.	Budget.		Report progress.		
Staff Development	Orient faculty.	Build knowledge base.	Faculty develops teaching model.		Begin training in new model.	
Curriculum development				Develop model lessons.		Write lessons.
Physical environment		Appoint student motivation committee.		Decorate corridors with student work.		
Student Attitudes	Appoint student fix-up committee.		Initiate first phase of student plan.			
Parents	Orient.			Train parents.		
Evaluation		Assess knowledge base.	Assess teaching model.			

County, North Carolina) decided early in their motivation project to produce a "Teachers' Guide to Student Motivation," to which all the faculty contributed. The guide included a research-based principle, followed by specific actions that teachers had tried and found successful.

- *Step Eight.* Later in the initiation stage, inform the community and the parents of your achievements. Parents' concerns again focus on the personal: How will this new program affect me and my children? The community's immediate concern is with funding: Where is the money coming from? Community people will also be skeptical about results: Is this one more fad?

- *Step Nine.* Throughout the initiation stage, the planners should monitor the planning process and the steps taken to accomplish their goals.

MAKING THE IMPLEMENTATION STAGE MORE PRODUCTIVE

The implementation stage is when you actually put the new program into effect. Researchers have identified several problems that complicate the success of this stage. They include (Fullen 1991, Louis and Miles 1990):

- *The innovation itself is of low quality.* Teachers do not perceive its need. It is either too simple (making little impact on learning) or too complex (resulting in teacher overload).

- *Communication is unclear, not timely, or not sufficient.* People need to be kept informed.

- *The innovation drains teacher time and energy.* Teaching itself is taxing and enervating. Adding the burden of change can result in increased stress.

- *Staff development is inadequate.* Many leaders foolishly believe that staff development is needed only at the beginning of a project. It is needed even more during the implementation stage, as teachers encounter problems.

- *Resources are inadequate.* The funds promised are not delivered; teachers are expected to implement the innovation without new texts, computers, software, and other materials.

- *Power sharing is nonexistent or superficial.* The planners are reluctant to share power. They feel an unprofessional jealousy about "our project."

To avoid these problems and to implement successfully, use the following strategies.

1. *Plan.* Maintain the evolutionary planning process. Develop a flexible schedule for the implementation stage, similar to the one shown in Figure 11-5.

2. *Include, communicate, and share power.* Work toward comprehensive involvement of all teachers, especially those who were initially resistant. Doing so will help you avoid the unfortunate division of the faculty into the "insiders" and "outsiders." Ensure that all planning meetings are open to all teachers and administrators. Keep everyone informed about problems and progress.

3. *Provide ongoing staff development.* Use external consultants initially, especially if technical expertise is needed. However, begin right away to train in-house consultants who can take over the training. Provide the staff development on a continuing basis, using quality time.

4. *Coordinate.* Even seemingly simple changes will probably impact upon several aspects of the school—the schedule, the curriculum, the teaching methods, and the physical environment. All these aspects need to be coordinated so that they support each other and move in the same direction.

5. *Act.* Keep in mind the action-orientation stressed throughout this chapter. Solve emerging problems.

Figure 11-5
DETAILED PLANNING: IMPLEMENTATION

	August	September	October	November	December	January
Administration	Check new materials.			Report on progress.		Report on progress.
Staff Development	Start intensive training.		Conduct problem-solving training.		Conduct problem-solving training.	
Curriculum development	Implement first unit.		Implement second unit.		Implement third unit.	
Physical Environment		Decorate study areas.		Decorate lounge.	Decorate library.	
Student Attitudes					Implement new peer-motivation program.	
Parents	Orient parents.	Continue parent training.				Update parents.
Evaluation	Evaluate staff development and unit.		Evaluate staff development, unit, and parent training.		Evaluate staff development, unit, and peer program.	

6. *Monitor and scan.* Monitor the innovation closely, but avoid premature summative evaluation. Be open to emerging problems. They are inevitable with any change.

7. *Monitor.* The mark of a successful leader is the ability to cope actively and successfully with problems. Louis and Miles (1990) point out that such passive coping tactics as these are ineffective: passive avoidance, doing business as usual, procrastinating, and shuffling people from job to job. Use instead such active strategies as vision building, sharing, evolutionary planning, re-staffing, and empowering people.

8. *Pace and be patient.* Avoid the dangers of overloading teachers by phasing in major innovations. You may need to take as long as three years to implement one major change.

FOR FURTHER READING

Fullan, M.G. 1991. *The new meaning of educational change.* New York: Teachers College Press. Useful research on the change process.

Louis, K.S. and Miles, M.B. 1990. *Improving the urban high school: What works and why.* New York: Teachers College Press. A detailed and very useful examination of the change process as it occurred at several high schools; but the implications seem sound for all schools.

REFERENCES

Cuban, L. 1988. A fundamental puzzle of school reform. *Phi Delta Kappan,* vol. 70, 341–34.

Fullan, M.G. 1991. *The new meaning of educational change.* New York: Teachers College Press.

Louis, K.S. and Miles, M.B. 1990. *Improving the urban high school: What works and why.* New York: Teachers College Press.

THE ADVISORY PANEL

Linda A. Bacon, Classroom Teacher and Vice President of the Pineallas Classroom Teachers Association, Largo, Florida.

Brenda DeRamus Coleman, Spanish Instructor, Lanier Academic Motivational Program, Lanier High School, Montgomery, Alabama.

Christine M. Sweeney, Professor of Education, Keene State College, Keene, New Hampshire.

Susan Walters, Certified Teacher and Site Coordinator of Extended Teacher Education Program, Wells-Ogunquit Community School District, Kennebunk, Maine.